The Learning Curve

The Learning Curve

Elevating Children's Academic and Social Competence

Judith Marks Mishne, D.S.W.

JASON ARONSON INC.
Northvale, New Jersey
London

This book was set in 12 point Bem by TechType of Upper Saddle River, New Jersey, and printed and bound by Book-mart Press of North Bergen, New Jersey.

Library of Congress Cataloging-in-Publication Data

Mishne, Judith Marks.
    The learning curve : elevating children's academic and social competence / by Judith Marks Mishne.
      p. cm.
    Includes bibliographical references and index.
    ISBN 1-56821-568-1 (alk. paper)
    1. Child development. 2. Parent and child. 3. Educational psychology. I. Title.
LB1117.M53 1996
305.23'1—dc20   95-16867

Manufactured in the United States of America. Jason Aronson Inc. offers books and cassettes. For information and catalog write to Jason Aronson Inc., 230 Livingston Street, Northvale, New Jersey 07647.

To my children,
Jonathan and his wife, Kate.

You must know that there is nothing higher and stronger and more wholesome and good for life in the future than some good memory, especially a memory of childhood, of home. People talk to you a great deal about your education, but some good, sacred memory, preserved from childhood, is perhaps the best education. If a man carries many such memories with him into life, he is safe to the end of his days, and if one has only one good memory left in one's heart, even that may sometimes be the means of saving us.

Fyodor Dostoyevsky, *The Brothers Karamazov*

CONTENTS

   Crisis   85

8 College: Late Adolescence and Early
   Adulthood—Consolidation and
   Stabilization   105

PART THREE
CHALLENGES TO PARENTHOOD

9 Homework and School Achievement:
   Whose Homework Is It Anyhow?   125

10 Working Mothers: Myths and Reality   143

11 Divorce: Changing Cultural Attitudes
    and Concerns   163

12 Parenting Gone Awry: Good Intentions
    and Unintended Consequences   187

13 Summary and Conclusions   211

    References   219

    Index   227

ACKNOWLEDGMENTS

With deep appreciation and regard I would like to thank a number of people and institutions for their help and support. I am grateful to Jason Aronson for his instantaneous, enthusiastic response to this book and his decision to publish it. My loyal typist, Richard Lenert, proved invaluable in providing moral support and prompt and skilled technical assistance.

I have been privileged to have had the opportunity to teach at a number of graduate school programs, namely the University of Chicago School of Social Work, the Columbia University School of Social Work, and the Smith College School of Social Work. For the last fifteen years my supportive academic home has been the New York University Shirley M. Ehrenkranz School of Social Work, a place that nurtures faculty and encourages research, writing, teaching, practice, and consultation. I am indebted to my colleagues and students who have stimulated questions and ideas.

In addition to teaching, I am involved in a part-time private practice in which I have worked for decades with caring parents, their children, and their children's teachers. I have also engaged in consultations at schools, social agencies, clinics, and residential facilities and have conferred with teachers and other staff committed to enhancing children's academic and social performance. These experiences have affirmed and reaffirmed how much can be accomplished—by parents and various professionals—to provide hope and ultimate mastery of the age-appropriate learning essential for growth and maturation. I offer my thanks to the children, adolescents, and professionals who have illuminated and helped me to refine the principles of parent guidance and of child and parenthood development that had been presented to me by my earliest teachers, supervisors, and mentors.

I particularly acknowledge what I have learned from the myriad of parents I have worked with over the decades. Their resilience, courage, and personal growth, in the context of parent-education groups or supportive treatment relationships, enabled them to move mountains and thereby to enhance their children's lives as well as their own. With a sense of acquired expectations and standards and a motivation to genuinely invest in the tasks of parenting, they gave themselves and their children real opportunity for learning and change, despite often severe early maladaptations or even failures. It is rarely too late to try to give oneself and one's child a second chance. Teachers, psychologists, social workers, and guidance personnel often facilitate that second chance for children and parents mutually engaged in a maturational process.

INTRODUCTION

The transformation of children and adolescents into confident adult workers and professionals is a major standard for judging a successful childhood, even though the age at which this transformation takes place can differ dramatically among communities as well as among ethnic groups and socioeconomic classes. Skills and knowledge necessary for adulthood are learned, but the length and nature of learning and dependency, and the substance of the learning, vary according to the culture. Schools are viewed as a major feature in children's lives not only because so much time is spent there but because schools are expected to perform roles almost commensurate with families in preparing children and adolescents for later life.

> Not only occupational preparation, but health care, self-discipline and social discipline, and becoming a good citizen are all expected, even demanded, from the educational experience. In fact, we have a tendency to see the school—and particularly the high school—as the principal remediator for social ills, and the inclusion of new courses in the curriculum as the best chance for prevention as well as cure. [Ianni 1989, p. 104]

Concerns about drug abuse, drinking, sex, AIDS, teen pregnancies, and adolescent suicides have stimulated counseling, and drug and alcohol education courses focused on sexual safe conduct, and parenting classes in the public schools. Courses in ethics are included in the curriculum of some schools, and although some of these courses are controversial, they are the consequence of contemporary social crises. Recently, violence in high schools in impoverished areas of American inner cities has stimulated courses in mediation and conflict resolution. Public schools are clearly locked into the issues that beset their communities, and programs and other efforts are attempted to offset the "shrinking of the extended family and the deterioration of the idealized model of the nuclear family" (Ianni 1989, p. 138).

Beyond references to the various crises in and about schools, I shall not attempt to address the multitudes of stressors and flaws in the public educational system; such a task is beyond the scope of this book. Schools differ regionally and by type of community, and some are plagued with high rates of student dropout, poverty, and parental unemployment, and with the impact of crime-infested neighborhoods. Other schools serve affluent families where materially overindulged children often appear estranged, undisciplined, inclined to risk taking, and irresponsible about work and academic performance. Delinquency and assaultive behaviors are observed across various socioeconomic and racial communities. Although private and parochial schools offer more protective settings, a multitude of serious problems afflict them as well (Lerner 1982).

The role of parents has been lost in the debates over political correctness, multiculturalism, the responsibilities of schools as social institutions, choice and voucher systems, public funds for private schools, teen sexuality, the two-career home, and the campaign for gender equality. Whatever the school programs and remediation efforts, parents' involvement is critical: schools cannot serve as the major institutional locus of child development, the agency responsible for socialization or acculturation in loco parentis. Twenty-five years ago, Dr. Seymour Lustman, professor of child psychiatry at Yale University and former chairman of Task Force IV, Joint Commission on Mental Health of Children, recounted the dilemma of education:

> Educators are an unappreciated, beleaguered, and underpaid profession: work fatigue, insecurity, frustration and consequent job change remain inordinately high; and the magnitude and complexity of the tasks at hand are increasing at a disconcerting pace. [Lustman 1970]

In the 1990s, the growing incidence of adolescent crime, violence, AIDS, drug use, suicide, multicultural awareness, and pregnancies has further stressed educators.

Freud suggested that mature, self-sustaining love of knowledge evolved from early, positive identification with parents and teachers. The concept of children's learning out of attachment and a wish to please the parents and thereby developing an independent desire for knowledge has been abbreviated in the following words: "Learning for Love to a Love of Learning" (Ekstein and Motto 1969). With these words in mind, I shall attempt to explicate the critical role parents can play in enhancing and elevating their children's academic and social learning, self-confidence, and self-esteem. In a posthumously published collection of essays entitled *Home Is Where We Start From*, D. W. Winnicott, a British child psychoanalyst, noted that child's experience in a particular family oriented him or her to all other human groups and endeavors. "Even when the peer group becomes a central influence, the basic social structure of the self, established in the family, continues to shape the interaction between the adolescent and the external world of the community" (Ianni 1989, p. 55).

Parents of all socioeconomic classes often feel overwhelmed, discouraged, even hopeless about guiding their children and confronting problems of living in their frequently compromised circumstances of marital conflict, single-parenthood, overwhelming work pressures, flawed schools, and adverse social milieus. I believe that such burdened parents can do more than they think if they can fortify themselves with knowledge, determination, and the will to pursue the struggle, and, if improvement is not forthcoming, to seek appropriate help from professionals.

Contemporary parents are bombarded by contradictions when they look for advice about understanding and dealing with their children. Parents want to do what is right for their children and to give them the best possible life, but they are often uncertain about what *is* best. Contemporary culture no longer provides a strong and clear message about how children should be reared. In addition, most people live apart from parents and extended family members who traditionally offered support, child care, and continuity in raising children. Most mothers are employed, in today's world of two-income households. These parents experience more pressures, less time for parenting, and often, greater uncertainty about the best approach. No cookbook recipe or set of rules covers the dilemma of working parents who must place their children, at younger and younger ages, in day care or with caregivers. Harried parents must try to compress affectionate and appropriate care of their children into their busy schedules.

One of the best avenues for understanding a child is by having a comprehension of children's development, and the corresponding parallel development of parents (Benedek 1970). The word "curve" in mathematics refers to a line whose path is traced by an equation that can be applied to any point on it. The "learning curve" of parents and children—the acquisition of knowledge and skill of both the child and his or her parents—ideally unfolds in a parallel and corresponding fashion.

> This two-way approach makes sense. As your child grows and changes, so do you. . . . Children don't go through their development alone. Parents go through it with them. Ideally, as children get older, parents *and* children learn to do things they couldn't do with each other and act in ways that weren't possible at earlier stages. It's not just a question of what "stage" the child is in, it's what "stage" are we in together. [Taffel 1991, pp. 44–45]

By way of emphasizing the parallel development and stages of the child's maturation, and the required changes in parenting, this book presents the learning curve of development from toddlerhood through young adulthood.

The child's age-appropriate tasks and mastery are presented in tandem with optimal parenting approaches, which are predicated on connectedness and empathic parental understanding, to facilitate parents' understanding of the child's ever-changing needs, fears, hopes, and wishes. Particular attention is given to helping parents support and elevate their children's general adjustment and self-esteem in the most important child-serving institution, the school. Because of the cultural changes and employment patterns of the 1990s, children are placed in a variety of school settings at younger and younger ages, and many remain there for a lengthy day that includes after-school care, to accommodate the employment of both parents.

Parents often know what they should do and want in some way to do, but may be paralyzed by internal or external inhibitions. External inhibitions may include conflicting advice and such pressures as financial and work-related demands. Internal inhibitions arise from excessive anxiety, trying too hard, or identifying too strongly with the child or with one's own parent. Anxiety about a child's negative reaction, including accusations that the parent does not love the child, is inhibiting to many parents. Often parents need permission to express their feelings and to exercise their own judgment. Useful parent guidance empathizes with parents and children and demonstrates how to support, or elevate, growth, by emphasizing the intimate connections between the emotional lives of children and parent. "It promotes insight into the meaning of behavior, so that child management is enhanced by an increased awareness. This is done through clarification of parents' and children's feelings, overt and covert behaviors, and concerns about limits and discipline. Parent guidance also helps parents find appropriate resources and offers guidelines about when to seek routine supports and facilities, special services, and therapy as needed.

The anticipated readers are professionals working with young people and their parents, as well as parents of children of all ages (preschool to college) who want to know about parenting and the developmental cycle of families. This book keeps several people in mind at once—namely, parents and children—since they are all going through some kind of developmental change. This developmental perspective brings the reader closer to comprehending the needs as well as the stresses of parents and children. Because of the transactional and interactional frame of reference inherent in notions of the developmental cycle of families, one becomes accustomed to thinking in multicausal and reciprocal terms about what is happening to all family members.

The parent-guidance approach appreciates the needs of children, as well as parents' needs, questions, and concerns. Simplistically blaming parents for children's problems adversely affects many therapeutic efforts and studies of parenting and child development. Children's needs cannot be sacrificed to the politics of the moment, to what is deemed "politically correct." Likewise parents' needs cannot be swept under the rug, when they seek information, advice, and direction in how best to provide for children in today's world.

Parent guidance is commonly viewed as a continuum, from simple information giving or education on one hand, to clarification, advice, and interpretation of feelings and behavior, on the part of children and their parents. The effort is to make the information and advice egosyntonic or acceptable, for the reader, the interested parent or professional working with parents who is committed to learning or teaching better parenting approaches. If a professional is to formulate recommendations that are palatable to and feasible for the parent, he or she needs to identify with the parents' situation, feelings, and previous efforts at understanding their child and in managing the inevitable struggles and challenges of the parenting process. Parent guidance attempts to enhance or elevate children's academic and social performance, and improve the parent–child relationship, by educating parents to normal developmental stages and phases of parent-and-child development, in order to clarify norms of behavior and age-appropriate tasks to help parents and professionals formulate or reformulate realistic expectations. This educational endeavor often entails dispelling popular notions that burden parent–child relationships and distort parents' otherwise reasonable efforts or good intentions to help their children.

In the aforementioned developmental context of child development and stages and phases of parenting, the major focus of this text is on preparing the child for the school experience, and, supporting the child in the lengthy home-based and school-based learning process, essential for academic success and social adjustment to facilitate the transformation of a child into a confident adult worker and professional. School is where children spend the majority of their waking hours, and this time span is on the increase as younger and younger children are placed in early day care and nursery programs, and older children are being enrolled in school-based early morning and after-school programs to accommodate working mothers. School is more than the site of academic and social learning, but rather the adjunctive child-care setting where youngsters may be placed from 7:00 A.M. to 5:00 P.M. Because of the recent increased prominence of school in children's lives, it appears timely to address school adjustment more thoroughly than has generally been done. School adjustment commonly occupies only a single chapter or section in existent parenting books. This appears insufficient in light of the enormous demands this form of care, education, and supervision deserves, given the actual time children now spend at school-based programs and in group care. Every chapter in this text devotes considerable time to schooling issues, the setting that furthers the sense of mastery, competence, self-discipline and positive self-esteem, that ideally originates in the home. The effort is to demystify child development and learning, children's nonverbal communications, the process of parenting, and even the therapy available, as needed, for parents and child. Vignettes and examples are provided in each chapter to help clarify these points. The style of presentation attempts to avoid any simplistic recipe or singular approach. "How to" information is offered to illustrate the issues and themes of each developmental age and stage, in order to deepen parents' and professionals' understanding of the manifest and latent content and messages in children's behavior and statements, and in parenting patterns.

PART ONE

"HOME IS WHERE WE START FROM"
(D. W. Winnicott)

1

Typical and Atypical Child Development

Parents and even professionals are often at a loss to determine which problematic behaviors in a child are transient and which are serious enough to require professional attention. Many of these problems become apparent in nursery school, elementary school, and high school—and even, much later, in college and graduate school. Pediatricians and family doctors may counsel parents to wait because he or she will "grow out of it," and this advice may be based on practice wisdom: Indeed the novelty of a school situation may create short-lived and only transient difficulties, whereas in other cases it signifies the advent of more serious underlying difficulties. Not infrequently, problems related to academic and/ or social adjustment are accompanied by a number of other signs or symptoms, suggestive of significant underlying problems.

Separation problems perfectly illustrate this point. Night fears and refusals to separate from parents and go to bed are common with 2- and 3-year-olds, and this generally abates in a matter of months. Parents are ill advised to capitulate to a toddler and surrender their expectation that he or she get to bed at a reasonable hour. Youngsters who are awake and demanding endless attention until the wee hours become increasingly tired, irrational, and quarrelsome; "patient" parents ultimately collapse and explode, and bedtime becomes a routine of apprehensiveness and anger, with parents and children in conflict. Parents must be kindly and firmly in charge because toddlers cannot be trusted to decide about bedtime, mealtime, and so on. Other mistaken parental indulgences include agreeing to lie down with a child until he or she falls asleep, and/or allow the child to sleep in the parents' bed. Mastery of the separation, and tolerance of frustration, are major requisites for a youngster's appropriate learning, growth, and mastery of age-appropriate tasks.

Some youngsters seemingly manifest no separation concerns until they are enrolled in nursery or day care, when they protest being left. Adequate preparation and explanations—and, at times, parents' staying until the child acclimates—should, optimally, reassure the youngster that he or she is not being abandoned, especially when parents return promptly, as promised, at school-dismissal time. Some children have temporary difficulty beginning any out-of-home program during specific life transitions, like a family move, divorce, or birth of a sibling. Here more preparation and support may be necessary and appropriate.

Because children do not develop in lock-step fashion, some youngsters may need more time at home before being enrolled in any kind of program. While early childhood programs typically begin at age three, the third birthdate is not an inflexible point of beginning for all. While some directors of preschool programs focus on parental readiness as more pertinent than the child's level of readiness, it is recognized that if parents feel a sense of compatibility with a program and trust the school, they are freer to let go.

The following factors are viewed as predictive of a child's readiness for a successful adjustment to an early childhood school:

1. a sense of confidence and security
2. a level of independence that enables a child to begin doing things for him or herself
3. a desire to explore and to have experiences outside the home
4. the ability to separate from the parent or primary caregiver
5. sufficient verbal skills to communicate with other children and adults
6. a beginning ability to relate to other children, to share, to take turns, to be part of a group
7. the ability to stay focused for a short period of time, to sustain an activity briefly in a goal-directed manner
8. physical development within the normal range
9. the ability to deal with the physical demands of the environment, for example, going up and down stairs, using the toilet, and so on. [Townsend-Butterworth 1988, p. 321]

Children may be uneven in their mastery of these abilities, but if they are significantly behind and unable to separate and communicate with teachers and peers by the age of 4, professional consultation is in order.

Some youngsters appear ready to separate in toddler-hood, and, after success in nursery school, manifest sudden separation problems at a later point, in elemen-tary school or upon promotion to middle or high school. Some children have unexpected problems in leaving home—for example, going to overnight camp—while some adolescents may evidence unanticipated panic and difficulty graduating into high school or leaving home for college. These later manifestations of separation anx-iety suggest some kind of regression and interfere with age-appropriate tasks, such that professional consulta-tion is indicated. It is not uncommon to note school-based problems, such as academic difficulty or decline in academic performance, additional to other signs or symptoms of distress. This can include friendlessness and social isolation, depression, fears and anxiety, aggres-sion, belligerence, and oppositional behavior. Problems in eating and sleeping and such habits as thumb sucking, nail biting, and bed-wetting are also red flags signaling that help is needed.

Parents generally provide the best they can, but fre-quently are preoccupied and overwhelmed by serious health, work, marital, and financial problems. Often well-intentioned but severely burdened parents note only the inconveniences their child creates, and thereby fail to recognize his or her underlying fears and despair. The degree of the child's inner suffering is often overlooked because it is frequently masked by belligerence, defiant behavior, and refusal to do schoolwork. Parents often recognize a discrepancy between their child's chronological and behavioral ages, and they can observe their youngster is suffering social disadvantages due to academic, social, or behavioral problems. It is important to seek professional consultation sooner rather than later, because the further behind the youngster falls, the greater the injury to his or her self-confidence and self-esteem.

It should be noted that academic underachievement affects all youngsters—those with limited ability, average ability, and superior ability. Intellectually gifted children can have serious school-based academic problems. Since the mid-1980s, American education has been said to be in crisis. Expectations for academic achievement have fallen lower than anyone can remember, and the best students especially have been affected by this in the most adverse ways (Lerner 1982). The benign neglect of the gifted child, who supposedly "can make it on his own," is now recognized as inhibiting the pace and level of these youngsters' learning, destroying their native curiosity, and undermining their motivation to achieve. Boredom and acting-out behaviors can arise out of a lack of teacher recognition and academic challenge. Special placement at varied grade levels, flexibly arranged, places children in specific subject-matter classes regardless of age. This tactic is preferable to wholesale skipping of grades or solitary, self-paced instruction; youngsters need peer interaction in the learning process. "It is not often that [students] [and in many cases even those who are of college age] have the self-discipline to pace them-

selves through an entire course without regular encouragement and feedback from an outside source" (Cohn
1988, p. 366).

The teacher is often the first to register complaints or
concerns. At times these communications upset parents
who feel that their child is being picked on, discriminated
against, or improperly evaluated. At times the teacher's
concerns may appear to be impatient complaints, signifying empathy with neither the child nor the parent.
Despite feelings that the school complaint might be exaggerated or erroneous, parents are empowered if they
do not ignore it and if they avoid doing battle, and instead
seek a professional evaluation by school-based clinical
personnel or an outside institution or child specialist.
This responsible follow-up affirms their parental sense of
responsibility, and serves to protect their child from any
hasty disciplinary or replacement action by the school.
Working parents often feel overwhelmed by requests
that they come in for parent–teacher conferences, but
prompt adherence to such a request is time well spent and
avoids later, often more time-consuming planning and
negotiation. Prompt action serves to solve smaller problems, which, if unattended, only escalate.

Some school faculty and personnel are more approach-
able than others, but despite the fit or lack of fit between
a parent and a teacher, it is important that the parent reach
for some degree of rapport and communication. If a
parent does not like and respect his or her child's teacher,
it is doubtful that the child will independently risk
trusting the teacher. Without trust, the child's learning

will be compromised. Schools have the power to make decisions about children's promotion, placement, and even inclusion in a program. Parents often complain about a sense of helplessness over stigma, labels, the placement of their children in Special Education classes, or the lack of invitation back, to a private or parochial school. The outside professional, in the person of a private practitioner or staff member of a social agency or mental health clinic, can often act as advocate or ombudsman to effect better communication between the school and the family. The child is best served when school personnel and parents, independently or with the help of school-based or community-based clinicians, form an alliance. Such a coalition of the adults significant to a child is a union in the best interests of the child.

2

Early Preparation
for School Adjustment

Parents are their children's first teachers, and what transpires during the earliest years is of critical importance in readying the child for out-of-home learning. Toddlers learn a great deal by identification and imitation, and complex concepts are transmitted during the first year of life. Speech and some level of communication are often acquired before a child is a year old. Under normal conditions, the more a child is spoken to, the more verbal and articulate the youngster will be. Explanations can be absorbed by even the preverbal child, as when the concept of *no* is presented. Parents prohibit the toddler from playing with dangerous objects, like stoves, matches, and electric outlets. In the same fashion, the very young child must accept the explanations, limits, and prohibitions at street crossings, the swimming area, the fireplace, and so on. Limits and explanations of other youngsters' rights and possessions are required—in the back yard, the tot lot, or any setting with other young children. In addition to articulating them, limits must be enforced. Too often, the aggressive child continues in combative behaviors in full view of the passive parent, who verbalizes protests but does not follow up the articulated prohibition. When the school setting complains about the unstoppable youngster, who is deaf to adult instructions or prohibitions, the hypothesis is that such behavior has mistakenly been ignored or tolerated in the home. Thereby the child enters a school situation disadvantaged by the inability to listen, follow instructions and directions, or easily form friendships.

Initiative and mastery begin early, when the toddler is permitted to do what he or she can independently. These independent acts include self-feeding, toileting, cleaning up toys, and self-dressing. Some parents, out of excessive fastidiousness, interfere with a youngster's efforts to self-feed and dress. Impatient to put things in order, they clean up after a child long after the youngster has the agility and coordination to put away toys. Toileting is a major educational task whereby bladder and bowel control becomes the child's, not the parent's responsibility.

During the second year of life the child is more focused on the pleasures and expectations of evacuation and elimination. Some parents mistakenly attempt to begin toilet training much earlier, by placing the child on a training chair immediately following a feeding or a meal. This interferes with a child's development of independence in toileting and too often conveys disgust about normal bodily functions. The organs of sex and elimination are close to each other, and thus attitudes developed during toilet training may affect sexual development. It is best to wait until the middle of the second year to begin actual training. A child's readiness is signaled by awakening from a nap dry and by dryness for a couple of hours during the awake periods of the day. Bladder capacity for control thus demonstrated suggests the child will respond favorably to being taken to toilet. It is not advisable to awaken a toddler at night to put her or him on the toilet. A performance achieved half awake is not a performance of independence. Generally bowel control in the second year precedes urinary control during the third year. Parents err if they are too permissive, or if they keep children in diapers beyond 2½ years of age. Calm, patient instruction is needed, and praise is important to stimulate a child's wish and efforts for cleanliness to please the parent(s). Diapers cannot be negotiated by the child independently, and thus training pants, which the child can handle alone by the middle of the second year, are essential for effective training. Change of residence, a new sibling, or family stressors can interfere with training or disrupt a child who has been clean and dry. Accidents or regressions are not uncommon in these circumstances. It is counterproductive to punish a child for soiling or wetting. Caring parents often err by making toddlers clean up their own soiled pants or forgo their story hour, favorite toy, or television program as a consequence for soiling, or wetting. Impatience, anger, spankings, and other punishments all have adverse effects in the power struggle or battle over the toilet. This can have repercussions in later academic learning; a failure to produce for the mother is often later translated into a failure to produce and do the work for the teacher. More serious difficulty is evidenced by enuresis. Primary nocturnal enuresis or continuous enuresis signifies that urinary control for a year or more has never been accomplished;

secondary enuresis or acquired enuresis indicates successful toilet training for at least a year, followed by a loss
of bladder control. Many authors think boys are twice as
likely as girls to evidence the symptom. Enuresis occur-
ring during the day or night can signify bladder infection,
a host of systemic illnesses, or childhood anger, anxiety,
gender confusion, and so on (Mishne 1993). Involuntary
defecation or encopresis is not due to organic defect or
illness but is a result of faulty training, mental retarda-
tion, or regression caused by psychological factors. Enuresis and encopresis signify a real need for professional
psychological intervention. Child specialists with a psychological perspective commonly disapprove of drug
therapy or behaviorist interventions such as DBT (dry
bed training) and urine alarm.

Parental patience, praise, explanations, and affectionate consistency are essential in teaching youngsters the
early tasks of self-care of the body and their belongings
and respect for the persons and possessions of others.
Management of anger and frustration is a major goal
during the first few years of life, when the child must
learn to wait and to tolerate delay and the lack of gratification of any and every wish or impulse.

Verbalization is one of the most critical components of
the parents' early educational efforts. The affectionate,
encouraging parent helps the child vocalize and express
him- or herself in words rather than in actions or temper
eruptions. Children first speak about their perception of
the outer world before verbalization of feelings, and the
capacity to articulate questions and ideas enables them to
better control anxiety, fear, or anger. The articulate child

is empowered to distinguish between fears, wishes, fantasies, and reality: verbalization leads to the solid integration of perception and cognition and acceptance of the reality principle. Nonverbal children commonly present gross motor discharge and an inability to contain feelings and affects. This can lead to impulsivity, hyperactivity, demandingness, and inability to sustain an activity in a goal-directed manner, all of which will immediately interfere with the learning and educational experience.

Beyond affectionate, warm, consistently maintained limits and expectations is the need for intellectual and creative stimulation. Children need tactile and sensory stimulation in the form of affectionate embraces and touching to stimulate their interest and pleasure in their body, their toys, and in the trusting seeking of new experiences. They respond to color, sound, and touch. A bleak and barren home depresses and deprives children; a chaotic and disorganized home overstimulates and confuses them. Suitable toys, music, and adequate play space are hopefully age-appropriate, whereby the child can engage in gross and fine motor activities such as running, tumbling, and bike-riding, and drawing, painting, and doing puzzles. Engrossment in active and imaginative play such as dressing up and various pretend games stimulates a child's creativity, capacities for reasoning and problem solving, and ability to focus on and complete a task or activity.

A child's play should never be undervalued. Play must be viewed as the equivalent of adult work. Play may be based on the pleasure principle, the desire to be big and grown up, or the need for mastery of something alarming, like recent surgery, whereby the child plays doctor over and over. The content and theme of a play activity commonly are not casual or interchangeable. Freud observed that all children behave like poets in their play because they create a world of their own. More accurately expressed, they transpose things into their own world according to a new arrangement of their choosing. Thus play is a leavetaking from reality and strongly parallels fantasy and daydreaming, all essential for creative self-expression.

Looking at picture books and being read to regularly and routinely stimulate the normally developing child to draw, color, and begin to recognize alphabet letters and numbers. Reading readiness occurs at vastly different ages. Parents' recognition of their child's ability is important, to avoid excessive demands and pressure when a child is not ready to read independently, or oversight when he or she is eager and ready to do so. Library story hours are good introductions to listening, as are discussions of the themes of stories. Reading requires far more than letter and word recognition; also necessary is the child's capacity to remember and to synthesize the meaning of the story, that is, tell it in his or her own words. This capacity is essential for later academic learning in a formal school setting.

It is not coincidental that children who have experienced parental loss, hostile parent–child ties, foster-home placement, or child abuse demonstrate severe academic difficulty. There was no learning to sustain the love of the parent, and no wish or ability to identify with or trust the parent. The negative imprint interferes with trusting or attempting to please other adults like teachers. The lack of basic trust and good self-esteem impedes a child's curiosity, creativity, or motivation to try new things and to persevere at a task. The vicious cycle continues as a youngster falls farther and farther behind and becomes angry and defiant as a defense against the shame of not being able to learn. Emotional attachment to a trusted adult is the prerequisite for successful learning.

In sum, educators and child specialists note how the young child engages in active efforts to master the environment and to identify and please persons and objects around them. The watchful and attentive child learns how and what to perceive through a complex process of seeing, touching, hearing, grasping, and throwing, imitating and identifying with the loved parents. Increasingly complex interactions, transactions, and cognitive development propel the child to learn, at first out of love for the parent. With greater separation and maturity the child progresses and learns in a more autonomous style and from an evolving love of learning.

3

Discipline: The Basis for Learning and Achievement

As defined by Webster, discipline is mental and moral training. Restraint and control are synonymous; the Latin root of the word *discipline* means teaching. The child is never naturally self-controlled, reflective, or reasonable. Disciplining a child requires parental self-discipline: calm, reason, and control in the expression of normal and inevitable anger and frustration. Myths have abounded about parent attitudes: parents should always feel loving and never angry at their children. Due to this mistaken view, parental anger often stimulates in the parent guilty feelings and self-recrimination, and thus, too quickly, an erasure of anger and disapproval, so that the child is not guided consistently toward appropriate behavior. Love is not enough. Good conduct must be taught and rewarded, and bad behavior must be responded to, not instantly forgiven or rationalized away simply because the parent understands the basis of the youngster's unhappiness. The child will rationalize away any and all unacceptable actions if that is the parental model. "The important gain for a child is in his regaining favor by improving himself, not by sidetracking the issues or questioning mother's loyalty (and love)" (Weisberger 1987, p. 58). Too often parents plead and cajole, expecting almost adult responsiveness from their young child. Parental patience then commonly evaporates, excessive anger is directed towards the child, parental guilt follows, and consequently the child continues in unacceptable actions like out-of-control or irresponsible behavior.

Discipline means teaching. It is not punishment or coercion. It gives children a key to choice; the ultimate aim is to make them responsible for themselves and their behavior. The long-range goal is a child's acquisition of self-control, and great parental effort is required to reach this goal. Children must be *taught* self-control, and this requires parental carry-through with consistent and firm expectations. The child must be stopped from hitting and other destructive behavior. This teaching requires firm parental intervention and making the child provide restitution in the form of apology, a portion of his or her allowance for breakage, and the like. Much will be learned from sensible, nonpunitive consequences. A child can be sent to her or his room to cool down after an explosion. He or she can be deprived of television and outdoor play, if they are incapable of playing with peers in a noncombative fashion. Eleanor Weisberger (1987) notes that this approach of clear, prompt consequences is positive because it makes children aware that they are expected to do better, implies that they have the capacity to improve, helps them see the connection between what they did and why they are being stopped, and gives them a chance to think things over without a fight. Youngsters cannot listen until they have calmed down; "time out" allows them to rejoin others when they think they can handle things. Removal of children from "the scene of the crime" and isolating them show that they cannot do whatever they wish without being stopped and helped to make better choices.

Limits and punishment should never be physically aggressive. Aggression begets aggression and only encourages children to move into more combative actions. When children are spanked, they feel entitled to be defiant and physically assertive themselves. Consistency, not everchanging rules, is essential.

According to Dr. Ron Taffel (1991), however, consistency is both overrated and outdated if parents fasten onto a particular method of child rearing that fails to retain a child's attention. Children will tune out their parents if there is no novelty, and Taffel warns that parents can become ignored background static if the script never varies. He recommends changing the parent/ child "dance," by doing such things as serving a mess of leftovers to children who grabbed and complained at mealtime and ignored the mother's elaborate efforts to present appealing and delicious meals. The goal is to curtail the same old monologues, lectures, and entreaties, and instead to creatively seize the child's attention. However the parents commands the child's attention, the essence is to convey to a youngster, over time, what is expected of him or her. One can't send mixed messages— expectations one day, and indifference to the same issue the next. Firmness is key, and a communication does or does not convey a parent's resolute expectation. Requests that are made offhandedly, or in a beseeching manner, are commonly ignored. Commands or direct orders should be used very sparingly if they are to maintain their effect. Dr. Rudolf Dreikurs (1992) suggests they should be reserved for real emergencies when danger is afoot and the child must respond immediately. On most occasions it is best to avoid direct commands. Holding the line is not easy for parents, especially when there are several children in the family, yet all efforts should be made, despite setbacks or a sense of discouragement. Encouraging the child to talk and express herself or himself is important but is sometimes carried too far, as in cases when limits are not applied in response to provocative, lawyerlike, argumentative children. Children will not respect parents if they know they can always win by wheedling, arguing, and throwing a tantrum. A child needs the safety and protection of limits and the knowledge that parents are indeed in charge.

Parental discipline means recognizing that there are many things you cannot make children do. "You cannot make your child eat, sleep, perform body functions, and when he is school age you cannot make him study and learn" (Weisberger 1987). There is simply no winning in the battle of the spoon, the toilet, or the book. Forced feeding can result in a child's promptly vomiting the food. Parents can eliminate much quarreling at mealtime by simply providing nutritious servings and pretty much ignoring the child's intake. They can limit snacks and desserts when the child ignores a major meal, but it's important not to make the meal a battleground. It is also important that a parent not become a short-order cook, preparing separate favorites for each family member. If a child misses a meal, matter-of-fact commentary is more than adequate; the child will ordinarily eat more heartily the next time. Children are not winning the battle when they refuse the meal; rather, parents win by refusal to engage in fighting and instead, remaining matter-of-fact. It is important not to equate food refusal with rejection of Mommy. A meal is but a meal.

If a child can't or won't sleep, some reasonable alternatives should be allowed such as quiet play in bed with books and/or cuddly toys. This lets the child wind down, and often she or he is fast asleep over the toys in a few minutes. Reading to a child is commonly soothing and provides a consistent bedtime routine. Very problematic patterns develop when parents feel forced to lie down with their children or allow their children into their bed. One can only make the bedtime routine, like the meal-time, as pleasant and calm a ritual as possible. Children will have individual patterns about food intake, sleep, and rest, which should not take over the home milieu. Protracted and bitter struggles with these routines or with achieving toilet training suggest a need for outside consultation and possibly some participation in parenting-skills groups available at most local Y's, churches, and temples. As will become apparent, the same principles applicable to bodily self-control apply to the issue of learning, when the child enters school. Parents' primary responsibility is to provide a calm, ordered environment that will allow children to responsibly handle these functions on their own.

Parents must intervene when children are antisocial

and aggressive; immediate prohibition is necessary, followed by helping youngsters to talk about their anger
when they are calmer. Expectations and standards must
be set: words, even angry words, are allowed, but hitting
and biting are unacceptable. Whining, messiness, and
dawdling are passive forms of aggression; each is grating
and infuriating to parents. Here again, parental calm and
consequences are required, to offset a kind of blackmail
that is commonly effective. Sometimes the dawdling
child must be left behind, perhaps with the sitter at home;
missing an outing may be the only way they will come to
see that they are undoing themselves and not the par-
ent(s). At times this is not possible, especially in households where mothers must rush to get to work promptly
after depositing children at school or day care. Effective
subsequent consequences in such cases may be earlier
bedtime and waking times until the child dresses and
breakfasts with normal alacrity. Being late to school and
having to face the teacher's censure is another realistic
consequence, which often requires a parent–teacher conversation to enlist the teacher's cooperation and understanding.

Refusal to comply with requests that are persistent,
whining demands by children can effectively curtail such
passive-aggressive demands. A parental refusal to give in
is most effective when coupled with permission for the
child to be direct and forthright in verbal expression of
anger and disappointment in the parent. If the parent sets
a tone that all things, including anger, can be discussed in
a reasonable manner, the whining commonly can be
surrendered.

The expectation for airing of feelings does not give license for the child to be verbally abusive. A verbal explosion is a close cousin to an aggressive temper tantrum: both require separation and a cooling-off period because genuine discussion and verbalization are not possible in the midst of a battle. Often parents must accompany young children to a quiet place like their room to be sure they do not hurt themselves or their things. Children feel safer when parents take control for a short time and let the children know they can rely on parental strength and calm to weather the storm.

The curtailment of messiness requires persistent follow-up and firmness. Cleanup has to be enforced with the young child. Parents must often set a hierarchy of priorities about what must be accomplished before permission is granted to go out and play, watch television, or socialize on the phone. Parents err greatly when they persist in cleaning up after their children, believing that they can do it thoroughly and more effectively than can the child. Children will then expect messiness and procrastination to pay off because passive refusal excuses them from doing the age-appropriate job. Such patterns interfere with carrying out later, age-adequate responsibilities in school, such as orderliness, cleanup, and handling the eventual tasks of homework and independently managed school responsibilities. The young children need help and instruction to clean and order their rooms whereas older ones need parental firmness, standards, and follow-through.

Letting children experience the natural consequences of their misbehavior is the most important method of preserving order. Comments, exhortations, nagging, and scolding only work temporarily, from without, when a child feels more or less forced into a certain mold of conduct. Parents must not continuously intervene to try to save their children from the unpleasant results of their actions. If a child dawdles and procrastinates when doing homework or departing for school, the parent must let the child experience the repercussions at school. A parent only perpetuates the problem by writing an excuse note to the school. Parents cannot raise children who will eventually develop inner acceptance of order if they attempt to spare the child discomfort. While you can empathize with their distress and express regret that they must undergo painful experiences, you must maintain a passive attitude about cause and effect. Consequences are distinct from punishment: consequences have an apparent logic that is inescapable and understandable to a child. "Telling him he cannot go to the movies if he does not eat his dinner has no logic; but if he does not come home from the movie on time, it is reasonable that he be told he may not go next week" (Dreikurs 1992, p. 68). Consequences are the natural result of misbehavior, but they are not retaliations. Allowing a child choice distinguishes between consequences and punishment. Yelling or sending unruly children from the dinner table to their room is a punishment, in contrast to stating firmly that children cannot remain with the family and disrupt it, and that they must go to their room until they feel able to behave properly. These vignettes demonstrate that the child has the power to alter the situation.

Limits are rarely effective when parents register

worry, irritability, or anger, and when they impulsively counterreact and inflict punishment. Punishments must be enforceable and realistic with a beginning and an end. No allowance, no television, or no phone privileges until further notice are vague, more threats than a reality. Commonly, children badger, putting pressure on parents to ponder "whether the child has learned the lesson, should I relent, was I too harsh," and so forth. Many children are skilled at bargaining and manipulating and can wheedle their way out of all restrictions, especially harsh ones made in haste. Parents are entitled to reserve judgment and delay their decision about what consequences are useful and fair. It is important to try to avoid humiliating children by publicly scolding and punishing them in front of peers and friends. Parental self-restraint, flexibility, and encouragement ensure retaining the child's attention. Even when limiting a child, one does best if care is taken not to reduce the child's self-confidence. The following phrases demonstrate parental expectations: "You make things seem harder than they really are; we learn by our mistakes; don't give up; I don't expect perfection, but you'll have to do your best" (Dreikurs 1992, p. 81).

Parents can limit comfortably in a spirit of mutuality. Admitting their own imperfections and similar mistakes at the child's age is fruitful only when the child is in a calm, receptive mood to listen. The parent has to demonstrate a wish to help, but at the same time should not relieve the child of responsibilities. A child may temporarily submit, when faced with arbitrary oppression as an expression of parental authority; but antagonisms will emerge, and covert defiance commonly ensues. It is always best to avoid negative command and rather, instead, emphasize the correct procedure instead of forbidding the incorrect.

The educational process of discipline requires that parents adhere to their role as kindly but firm adults. When children violate limits, parents must not become argumentative, excessively angry, or verbose. It is also important not to register amusement or covert pleasure at a child's spunky defiance, if one doesn't want to face the same thing over and over. It is not necessary to be drawn into lengthy discussions about the fairness or unfairness of a given restriction, nor is it necessary to give lengthy lectures on why one can't hit a sibling. When children exceed a limit or break a basic rule of conduct, their anxiety mounts: they expect some parental response and restriction. When parents talk too much, they convey weakness and uncertainty. It is important to communicate with offending children in a way that does not cause them to lose face. Children do not benefit from spanking, and allowing a child to hit the parents is *most* ill advised.

In disciplining children it is important to stimulate development of their conscience, and their sense of fairness, values, and inner restraint. Spanking relieves guilt too easily; when children feel they have paid for misbehavior with the spanking, they feel free to repeat it. Children develop what Selma Fraiberg (1959) called a bookkeeping approach to misconduct; this attitude permits them to misbehave and go into debt on one side of the ledger, paying off in weekly spanking installments.

RAMIFICATIONS FOR THE
EDUCATIONAL PROCESS

Overall, it is important to recognize that effective parental discipline results in a number of internal achievements. Discipline and guidance develop in the child, along with the capacity for trust in others and self-trust, the capacity for autonomy as well as for accepting control by others whenever necessary, and the capacity to develop initiative and a working conscience (Ekstein 1969b). These achievements are the basic ingredients that make for learning readiness in young children. Without these achievements, children enter school defiant, distrustful, and untrustworthy. Their initiatives will be destructive and defiant and will distort any constructive capacity to learn. Such children develop a stance of apathy and indifference.

In developing self-discipline, teachers have specific advantages that parents do not have. Teachers generally can be more objective and rational in their approach. Parent–child ties commonly cause parents to be more emotional, easily aroused, and angered, or more sympathetic and indulgent. Teachers are less emotionally invested in each youngster; they can be fairer than parents and note the needs of individuals and of the group. In the classroom teachers can be less personally embroiled because they are responsible to the class as a whole; in such a setting, children have a powerful incentive to seek group approval and prestige. Teachers can use the group to develop each child's insight into the causes, logical and illogical, of everyone's behavior and the consequences of each person's actions on the other (Richardson 1969).

PART TWO

THE SCHOOL EXPERIENCE

4

Nursery School: Passion, Pretend, and Practicing

NORMAL DEVELOPMENTAL AND MATURATIONAL ACHIEVEMENTS

Three-Year-Olds

While there is great variation among healthy children, educators and child specialists agree on various aspects of age-appropriate achievements. The average 36-month-old preschooler demonstrates specific physical and physiological landmarks, and these include specific maturation of the brain, which results in increased coordination of eye, hand, and small muscles. Thus 3-year-olds are able to handle crayons, paints, markers, puzzles, pens, and pencils. Their drawings are hardly realistic: figures of people will be missing limbs, ears, and the like; but a person, a tree, or a flower may be discernible. Likewise, some youngsters begin to print their name. The letters may be up- or downhill and of various sizes but nevertheless recognizable, despite the common age-appropriate reversals of *B*s, *D*s, and the like. The child's efforts should be praised, and the parent should not push for more mature productions.

This physical maturation and coordination is also apparent in 3-year-olds' ability to feed themselves and, in a rudimentary way, to handle a fork or spoon. Self-feeding can be a messy process, but independent handling is more important than the droppings on the floor and the mess of chocolate pudding over the child's face. Drinking from a cup is important, as is prior weaning from the bottle, including at bedtime. It is common for a 2½- or 3-year-old to regress and demand a bottle again, if and when a sibling is born. It is helpful, however, not to indulge children in this regression and to emphasize instead, their status as an older big sister or brother. The reality principle distinguishing between infants and nursery-age children should not be erased. Hence bottles are only for babies and toddlers.

Toilet training has ideally been achieved, albeit with occasional accidents. Being out of diapers and able to independently manage bladder and bowel control are major achievements. Two-and-a-half-year-olds and three-year-olds normally have the bladder and sphincter control to remain clean and dry for extended intervals, and because they sleep in a bed, not a crib, they should be expected and allowed to get up from bed to independently toilet themselves. A child is confused if they are in underpants by day and diapers by night. The message is ambivalent: "Be big and a baby at the same time." Keeping a child in diapers at this age keeps a child dependent and tied to the mother. Protracted maternal involvement in the toilet overstimulates children, as the mother is taking care of too much and doing too much for them. Mothers who delay children's training in this area delay it in other areas, such as teaching them to feed, dress, and wash themselves. Belated acquisition of these skills stifles ambition and initiative and does not appropriately ready youngsters for group care.

Recommendations about feeding and toilet training have undergone definite cycles that have swung between extremes of rigidity and permissiveness. Overpermissiveness leads to excessive tolerance of sucking, soiling, and masturbation. Although the philosophy of permissiveness has been lengthy, dissatisfaction with it has grown. Thus, decades ago Dr. Benjamin Spock revised his famous book on baby and child care to counteract a growing tendency toward overpermissiveness. Protracted solicitousness and maternal overinvolvement in feeding and toileting can lead to serious problems that are simply the other side of the coin of overcontrol and overdomination. Maternal overinvolvement is always characterized by domination or indulgence, and both produce rebellion and immaturity characterized by disobedience, tantrums, and demandingness.

Any immaturity about self-care of the body is associated with symptoms such as shyness, fatigue, short attention span, infantile speech patterns, and inability to follow directions. These symptoms commonly translate into the following complaints from first-grade teachers: "He does not finish tasks or complete and follow directions; he cannot work alone at his desk and is incessantly moving about, is easily distracted, cries and gives up too easily, is fearful and clings to the teacher." Such emo-

tional immaturity is characterized by a low tolerance for
frustration such as the need to wait one's turn and is accompanied by minimal self-control or self-direction.
School is experienced as too hard and the child feels no
responsibility to do the work. The overindulged child
generally has experienced gross inconsistency, punctuated by hostility and blowups between parent and child.
Enough is never enough, and there develop neverending
cycles of insatiable demands, which repeatedly escalate
into parent–child conflict after excessive overindulgences
(Kessler 1966). Independent mastery and care of the body
in feeding and toileting and care of one's drawings and
toys come from firm and patient parental expectations
punctuated with praise, affection, and encouragement.

Parent–child relations at this age are often somewhat
strained by the youngster's seemingly intense preference,
even passionate attachment, to the parent of the opposite
sex. This preference can be especially trying in one-
parent homes where the female child yearns for contact
with the noncustodial parent, commonly the father.
Preferential affection is long and taxing and is often
accompanied by endless practicing of imagined future
roles and identities as, not uncommonly, the partner or
spouse of the parent of the opposite sex. Thus, girls of age
3 declare they will grow up to marry their fathers, and
boys of similar age declare the same marital plan for
themselves and their mothers.

Beyond imaginative and pretend games, nursery-age
youngsters demonstrate ever more complicated abstract
and symbolic play. At this age, children demonstrate
early ego ideals in the form of kings, princesses, cow-

boys, dancers, superstar athletes, and the like. They love to dress up and pretend that they are adult mommies, daddies, kings, queens, and teachers. There is increased interest in social interaction with peers, and increased socialization skills, including more sharing, taking of turns, and animated conversations and activities, normally occur. This increased interest in other children corresponds to the child's greater comfort with separations from mother, who is etched firmly in the child's memory. Mother is beloved, when she both gratifies and frustrates the child. This secure tie enables the well-developing child to expand the above-mentioned peer relations and to increasingly appreciate nuances of behavior and subtle aspects of identity in others. Despite this expanding attachment to peers, children still depend primarily on parents for pleasurable recognition of achievements.

The 3-year-old's parent is relied on to provide patient support of the child's progressive development and pleasure and comfort with the child's gender identity. Parental patience is often taxed but empathy must be provided despite the child's erotic-like, passionate attachment to the parent of the opposite sex. Parental empathy must be accompanied by the containment of any type of seductiveness by either parent. Privacy for all, when toileting, bathing, dressing, and so on, must be maintained. The young child will be overwhelmed and overstimulated by parental and sibling nudity, which can inspire feelings of inadequacy by comparison, as well as feelings of overwhelming excitement. The appropriate nursery school will have similar boundaries and divisions to afford privacy by gender in use of bathroom facilities; the age-appropriate sexual curiosities at this age must be talked about, rather than acted out.

Four-Year-Olds

Along with bladder and bowel control and increased fine and gross motor coordination, children experience some decrease of passion and attachment to the parent of the opposite sex. Parental figures may appear in the disguised form of heros and heroines as fantasy role models when children practice being grown up; but pretend games, increasingly solid reality testing, improved impulse control, and frustration tolerance appear by age 4. Real social judgment should be apparent as the child demonstrates accurate, conflict-free perception and memory.

By this time, well-developing youngsters are capable of complex experimentation and practice to demonstrate their greater independence. Figuring things out on their own and visiting at friends' homes are reflective of greater autonomy, which is accompanied by expanded tolerance for more lengthy separation from the parents. These achievements are based on increased self-esteem and a more stable sense of the self, which facilitate socialization and resilience in social situations. No longer is the child's sense of self threatened by the ups and downs in peer interactions. Along with pleasure at outside approval, children enjoy more confidence when competing in social situations; winning and losing are taken more in stride. There is demonstrable love, appreciation, and attachment to extended family members, teachers, and a widening circle of peers.

PARENTING PATTERNS

These developmental achievements are supported by parental encouragement and pride in the child's maturation. By this time children can sublimate, or alter, their mode of expression. They can demonstrate progress and maturation in how they handle anger. For example, they can be helped to choose to draw an angry picture rather than collapsing in a tantrum. Such achievement receives parental rewards in the form of praise and approval, as the parent revels and participates in the child's increased self-control, and cognitive and social abilities. By the age of 4, children can accept parents' honest communications about stressful family events.

No longer will parents initiate all the play and games. Allowed to take initiative, children at this age will assume it, for example, in retelling favorite stories and fairy tales. Children often become voracious for invented tales as they approach the ages of 4 and 5; stories contribute to role models and provide a subtle moral education in a way that abstract ethical concepts cannot (Kleiman and Rosenfeld 1980). Bruno Bettelheim (1976), discussing the use of stories and fairy tales, noted the following benefits: entertainment, the arousal of curiosity, and the stimulation of imagination. Fairy tales help develop children's intellect and assist in clarifying their emotions,

because such stories deal with universal human problems.

The need for heroes is critical, and there are long-range
consequences when parents are negative role models.
Neglectful or overly aggressive parents make the children feel they deserve no better, and this leads to low
self-esteem, a confused self-concept, lack of confidence,
anger, and a sense of victimization. Major parental
change and, commonly, professional help are required to
alter this serious imprint on young children, who erro-
neously blame themselves all too often. Early poor self-
esteem is worsened by almost inevitably poor adjustment
at school. Even conscientious and loving parents can
impair their youngsters out of anxiety, overprotectiveness, and excessive pressures to perform. Wanting
their children to succeed, caring parents may feel undue
anxiety over the uneven development of their youngsters, who are age-adequate despite an irregular array of
abilities. Early-childhood testing for nursery acceptance
unhinges even the most sophisticated and knowledgeable
of parents. Some preschool programs are extremely
competitive in their admission decisions, and the testing
results often disqualify adequate candidates who "froze"
on the day of the school interview.

Vignette

Jennifer, 3 years old, is a beautiful and outgoing little
girl, verbal and animated, blonde, blue-eyed, and di-
minutive in size. Her parents are Protestant, upper

middle class, well educated, and knowledgeable. They had great difficulty conceiving a child. The mother suffered three miscarriages and an ectopic pregnancy before the parents sought in vitro fertilization to maintain a pregnancy. Despite the low success rate of this procedure, Jennifer was conceived, and the pregnancy went easily. Amid the relief and joy at finally having a healthy child, the parents experienced continual anxiety about her progress and development. (Subsequent in vitro attempts for a second child failed, and Jennifer would be their only child.)

Jennifer was often intimidated by boisterous youngsters at various play groups and gym programs. She was afraid to try new activities like swimming and appeared to recoil from parental pressures to excel. The more her parents pressured and urged her to behave aggressively and actively, the more she held back. She seemed afraid to try for fear of failing and disappointing her parents more. As Jennifer was reaching the end of nursery school, her parents became anxiously engaged in visiting various private elementary schools. They expressed grave doubts about how Jennifer would perform in school-admission interviews and tests. Their anxieties created a self-fulfilling prophecy: their very intelligent and artistic child performed badly, froze, or resisted some school interviews, would not separate from her parents, and, on the testing, was scattered and erratic in performance.

The parents sought some short-term parent guidance and therapy for Jennifer. They opted to keep her in nursery school an extra year to lessen the pressures that they recognized but could not restrain themselves from applying. The support of professional help and the extra year in nursery greatly eased Jennifer's and the parents' worries. The parents received reassurances about and clarifications of their youngster's basic ability and could surrender their pressuring efforts. This helped to free Jennifer, who had held back, preferring not to risk efforts at greater maturation. The child's play therapy initially revealed the desire to stay little. Over time as progress was made, confidence and a wish to grow emerged.

By the time that testing was scheduled a second time, Jennifer's performance had greatly improved. She was admitted into several very good school programs. She was not admitted to two of the most competitive settings, and this is viewed as having led to Jennifer's self-protective differentiated testing performance at various schools. She sensed a more aggressive tone and demeanor at these programs during her school visits and clearly opted for less-threatening school settings. Her therapist's view (supported by psychological testing) was that Jennifer's intelligence qualified her for the most rigorous of schools, but her temperament and reluctance to aggressively compete suggested that she would do her best in a less-demanding setting. This young child showed her capabilities in different ways at different schools and thereby got herself enrolled where she felt most comfortable. The parents' modified views of the wide range of options enabled them to alter their expectations and to improve the parent–child–school fit.

THE BEST PARENT–CHILD–SCHOOL FIT

Despite current local and national debate about public education for nursery-age children, nursery at present remains a private-school option based on parental choice. Head-start programs or community funded preschool programs are the only options for families without financial resources for private nursery settings. Private nurseries can be found attached to YMCAs, churches, and temples; many exist as freestanding, independent programs. The range and variation of nursery schools can be enormous, especially in large urban areas and in communities with extensive suburbs. Parents face a daunting task in making the best selection. They commonly begin by considering cost, location, and the number of hours provided for nursery care and education. Visits and information seeking are time-consuming but necessary tasks to avoid poor selections that might ill effect a child.

Whatever the needs of children and parents, certain variables apply in all cases. Parents must attempt to determine the philosophy and orientation of the program, the adult–child ratio, the level of training of teachers and school director, the space and physical plant, atmosphere and cleanliness, play areas and play equipment, group size, routine activities, extra activities such as school outings to children's activities, museums, and plays, and meal- and rest-time arrangements. Parents should visit, investigate, and not hesitate to ask questions in their research efforts. Parents with restricted financial resources may feel that they have few if any choices, but this perception is often inaccurate. Many institution-based programs offer a sliding fee in accord with family income.

Parents attempt to pick a school that they can trust, based on the apparent atmosphere, style, and philosophy. Those seeking a more structured program may well prefer a Montessori school, whereas others may opt for a more relaxed atmosphere. Some parents value sports and athletic activities or science activities, while others prefer a setting that emphasizes the arts, with heavy emphasis on music, painting, and drawing. Whatever the program, the teacher–child ratio is most important as is the teachers' level of training and experience.

To be avoided are unlicensed programs staffed by untrained caregivers and programs that put little premium on cleanliness, suitable toys, and activities. Such settings are often parking places where children are deposited on an almost cash-and-carry basis. In these inadequate programs, too many children mill about in a large room where no social structure is maintained.

> The recommended adult/child ratio for preschool (3- to 5-year-olds) is one to seven or eight children. Far better some of us think, is a one-to-four ratio in which one primary caregiver or teacher is available to four children. In a good group program for pre-school children, one can see the centrality of the adult, as children in the course of a single hour move from peer group play to the adult, "touching base," returning to an activity or to a private pursuit. [Fraiberg 1977, p. 85]

In an ideal program, an adult is always available for conversation, for reading a story, for comforting a distressed child, for enhancing a talent or an interest, and for responding to each child's personality and individual needs.

Since nursery is a child's first encounter with school, parents hope to make the best possible selection and thereby ensure a positive beginning in the long educational process. It is unwise to think that the preschooler is so young that the school does not matter. This first experience out of the home and into a more structured learning situation sets a basic tone about teachers, education, the peer-group experience, and children's sense of themselves. The optimal nursery experience will expand children's curiosity and stimulate a desire for more new experiences, independence, and learning. Children will feel safe separating from parents, and their ability to relate to other children will expand. This experience demonstrates that choices are possible; it provides an arena that nurtures children's emerging cognitive, social, and athletic capabilities. The good nursery experience readies children for the demands of formal education.

5

Elementary School: Latency— The Age of Industry

NORMAL DEVELOPMENT AND MATURATIONAL ACHIEVEMENT OF THE LATENCY-AGE CHILD

During the age of 5 or 6 until the onset of puberty, the child is said to be in the latency period, a time of dormant sexuality and a period when growth and maturation are such that moral and ethical concepts are understood and incorporated. Children ideally begin to identify with parental and community values and begin to possess inner controls rather than totally relying on adult authority figures. Complicated social, religious, and ethical standards are internalized. With the essentially complete development of the central nervous system, normal, average children are ready for learning advanced skills such as reading and math.

Because children now have increased capacity for reality testing, tolerance of frustration, memory, and the presence of a conscience, they can synthesize the outer demands of authorities with their own self-expectations. Relationships are more mature and empathic, with evidence of altruism and consideration of others, as children increasingly relate to nonfamily out of a greater separation from parental figures. Teachers, peers, and other adults are of increasing interest, and children demonstrate a capacity for intimacy along with more stable self-esteem and confidence based on joy at mastery of increasingly complex academic, social, and athletic activities. These significant personal gains and abilities are predicated on the parents' provision of love and approval. Parents also demonstrate their commitment to values and expectations; they give permission for children to increasingly emancipate and test newly acquired activities while forging their own identity. Dr. Charles Sarnoff, a child psychoanalyst who specializes in latency, writes: "Latency provides the period of time in which children can learn the complicated skills needed in the society. . . . It is a period where the child consolidates his image of himself in relation to the world" (Sarnoff 1976).

During this period the child is ideally eager to get out into the world of school and peers to accomplish many social, academic, sports, and play activities. The children's universe is no longer the home but the neighborhood, the school, and the wider community. They have finally come to recognize that there is no workable future within the womb of the family, and they apply effort to acquire new skills. Children seek and thrive on recognition by the peer group, and they enjoy the rewards of effort at school or in any learning activity such as extra lessons (dance, music, art) or sports.

Because of brain and neurological maturation, normal children have reached a level of development that permits greater autonomy. The neuromuscular apparatus is ready for the challenges of sports, and additionally there are cognitive strategies whereby they can better control their environment. Operational thought, organized memory, and better self-control result in logical and more structured thought processes, capacity for symbolic learning, and fantasy production. Energy abounds as these preadolescents race, tumble, climb, swing, skate, play ball, master academics, and engage in complicated, organized team sports. The ability to formulate or follow rules is not easy, and children go through stages of making, changing, and breaking rules. Sometimes they are quite strict with others about rules of games or acceptable behaviors, and they develop group codes that have consequences for cheating and tattling. Because of operational thinking and abstract conceptual memory organization, there is improved reality testing and the ability to reach an abstract rather than a rote memory level. Moral development is ideally more firmly in place, and the capacity to verbalize feelings replaces earlier impulsive aggressive expression. Failures make children feel inferior to peers, and a wish for inclusion and peer approval compels children to do the right thing.

Latency-age youngsters define themselves in doing things. They are what they do, and they commonly delight in showing and telling about their achievements, whether a baseball-card collection, a baseball play, their swimming speed, or the story or picture that earned teacher approval. Although approval or disapproval of teachers and parents remains most important, peer judgment becomes increasingly significant for a child's self-esteem. Visual–motor and auditory–visual integration have matured by age 7; thus the child can concentrate for longer periods. Time management is possible, and decisions may be made about projects, play, and independent management of school work. Often parents and teachers' helpful interference is resented; children want permission to make choices, decisions, and even mistakes on their own.

During the latency years the child has a wealth of fantasy. Creativity is evident in the use of arts and crafts materials, writing, and dramatic play. Commonly these creative capacities seem to recede just before puberty, because of stresses connected to bodily change, the expansion of logical thinking, and more sophisticated verbal communication. Some talented children may continue to be creative, even at the price of some social isolation and outsider status (Buxbaum 1980).

TASKS OF PARENTING

Latency-age children's freedom from sexual strivings is reinforced by their partial separation from the parents, the objects or persons that are young children's first sexual subjects of attention. In latency the parents must have an ability to let go, to separate from and to surrender the child to teachers, who act as guardians of quiescent sexual and aggressive experiences. Teachers are enforcers of independence from parents and organizers of systematic skills. Releasing children to the teacher and the learning process is a move into *part-time parenthood,* made to stimulate children's independent industry and learning process. Parents normally use sets of references as aids in adjusting to the child's changing identity. They rely on tangible signs of maturation such as visible physical changes and acquisition of skills. They follow ritualized customs of child rearing and act on their positive and negative identifications with their own parents. Parents struggle to transform themselves to meet this developmental phase as the child moves away, seemingly at times to reject the parents, in the move toward greater independence. Parents must be flexible enough to allow their ideas and demands to assist the child in this transition, strengthening, amplifying, and making concrete the child's self-image as a member of a student body and an independent achiever. Supportive and secure parents help mediate this double-directed course, as children struggle to negotiate both home and family life and the outer world. The move out of the family nest absorbs the child's psychological and cognitive resources. The efforts to separate, control the immediate environment, learn, make friends, and succeed in work and play are enormous challenges. Ideally the child changes, and neither parent can remain the same. While there are regrets about no longer being exclusively needed, parents ideally also take great pride in the child's advancement.

When latency does not unfold normally, there is a common theme of inability to let go, be it by the child, the parent, or both. For many reasons, some, if not all in the family are unprepared for this age-appropriate maturational step. Difficulties may be manifest in behavioral problems, poor academic achievement, and over-reliance on parental figures, friendlessness, or actual fears and resistance to school attendance. If these problems do not abate in fairly short order, consultation with a pediatrician and the child's teacher is in order, and contact with a professional child therapist may be necessary. Professionals trained to work with parents and young children practice as private psychotherapists and as staff members in social agencies or mental-health clinics. These professionals have been trained as clinical social workers, child psychologists, child psychiatrists, or child psychoanalysts. A child's school is often a good resource for referral, if a pediatrician cannot perform this service.

The seeking of prompt help is critical, lest children fall behind their peer group and thereby exacerbate the already existent sense of failure, and emerging poor self-esteem. The lag in learning is significant: children need to understand the progression of academic concepts to meet the required classroom expectations the next day, week, and month of the school calendar. If lost or confused now, they will only feel more lost and overwhelmed in the weeks and months ahead, fearful of the work that is next presented. There are few miseries of childhood more painful than sitting in a classroom, feeling confused, and lost, and unable to do the work. Despite defiance, belligerence, and rebellious statements that "I don't care," it is the rare child who really does not care. The defiance and manifest indifference are really a defensive cover for mortification over a sense of incompetence and failure.

Academic achievement is not the only measure for evaluating a child's school adjustment. Some youngsters with good to excellent grades are, nevertheless, unhappy, anxious, and suffering low self-esteem. These symptoms may relate to serious social problems such as an inability to make and keep friends. The scapegoated child, the unpopular one, the child who feels rejected and always the outsider is a youngster in real distress. It is a mistake to dismiss social maladjustment as one of those things that he or she "will grow out of." Social skills are a requisite for normal confidence and self-esteem; problems in this area require parental attention to the same degree as does academic difficulty. No rationalizations or dismissal of the importance of social relationships comforts or helps the child. Parents must try to place themselves in their child's shoes, to empathically comprehend the pain their child is experiencing. Once alerted, parents can sometimes help their child alter this situation. However, on many occasions, the parents may be as helpless as is the child, and outside help is necessary. Trying to push the lonely child into new social activities and clubs to help them connect with peers is usually a failure and only inflicts more pain and a sense of despair. If a child cannot connect with neighborhood peers and school classmates, there is no basis for expecting miraculous change in a new scouting group, art class, or camp setting. The child simply takes the same problems of inhibition and aggression into the new situation. Outside changes will not alter the child within, and old patterns cannot help but be repeated. Rather than expose a child to yet another rejection or failure, parents are wise to seek professional guidance.

Parents may correctly recognize that various family problems may explain a child's school-based academic and behavior problems and social estrangement. It is unwise to delay seeking help for a child until family-based problems are corrected. The latency-age child must be helped as quickly as possible to function age-appropriately and as successfully as possible in school, despite whatever is going on in the home. Short of extremes that result in placing a young child out of the home, distressed, divorcing, ill, or unemployed parents can be helped to attend simultaneously to their own needs and to their child's. The child cannot wait until family life settles down, since the required skills of latency are enormous, and once a child falls behind, he or she may feel permanently behind. Despite symptoms and unhappiness, the child must be helped to maintain a progressive line of development. Significant regression or arrest is serious given the rapidity and enormity of children's developmental changes. Being out of sync with one's peers, and unable to keep up the required learning, creates a sense of stigma and feelings of inadequacy. Hearing older children recount their earliest memories of failure in the lowest primary grades, those of us who work with children and adolescents realize how much better it would have been if help had been secured promptly. Many agencies and clinics provide crisis and "prompt response" services in an effort to offer preventative and early intervention that help to avoid further deterioration and failure.

ESSENTIAL HOME-BASED STRATEGIES TO SUPPORT SUCCESS IN SCHOOL

Full-time elementary-school attendance is a major developmental step that must be taken seriously. The child's attendance and investment in school are the equivalent of an adult's work. Making the child feel secure and responsible about attendance, punctuality, and appropriate handling of homework begins in the first grade. What occurs in the lowest grades begins what are often lifelong work patterns and behavioral and character traits. Parents are mistaken if they underestimate the importance of daily attendance and punctuality in the lower grades. Ideally parents provide a set of expectations that attendance is not a matter of whim or preferences, subject to choice or ignored, if one is not feeling perfect. When school is missed, return often becomes an anxiety-producing situation; re-entry, and catching up, and reconnecting to the peer group, the teacher, and the academic work feel, for many, like an overwhelming challenge.

Structure and routines at home prepare the child for the structure and routines in the classroom. Getting up in ample time for a relaxed dressing and breakfast schedule is important; the child who feels rushed and disorganized enters the classroom in a disoriented state and is unable to attend to the work at hand. Appropriate awakening time is predicated on enough rest and a reasonable bedtime the night before. It is dismaying to hear about various forms of home-based chaos whereby children are dragged from bed, pushed into their clothes, and hustled off to school, tardy or almost late, without breakfast, or any comfortable leavetaking. Assuming that the parent(s) arise promptly, so should the child; and the child's own alarm clock, provided early, helps in acquiring skills in time management. Awareness of time, with an appointed hour to be dressed, have the bed made, and be ready for breakfast is a good pattern to begin early in life.

Some children become anxious about separation and displace their anxiety onto the issue of attire; they thus express anxiety and indecision about what to wear to school. Tactics such as putting out clothes the night before may serve as an aid but not a solution. Because the original anxiety is not dealt with, it can reappear, and the clothing selected the night before may be rejected as "all wrong." Dawdling and complaints about clothing may mask hidden concerns often connected to separation, performance anxiety, and perfectionist strivings for superior academic achievement. Parental reassurances about parent–child reunion at the end of the school day, and about approval of a child's best work efforts even if imperfect, do more to allay fears than do policies over clothes selection. It is crucial for the parent to take the time to listen on several levels to what the child says, and to what might be the underlying concern. Complaints about clothing and others' possession of toys and games often mask a child's social problems: "Everyone else but me has a leather jacket." "Everyone but me owns that video game." Instant gratification, with purchases of items demanded, never gives a youngster the missing sense of confidence and assurance necessary to build solid peer relationships.

Homework is a critical issue even in the early grades

and commonly becomes the new battleground, echoing the earlier battles of the spoon, toilet, and bedtime hour. Procrastination, avoidance, excessive frenzy and anxiety, dependent demands for help, sloppiness, and superficiality in handling assignments are typical maladaptive reactions to homework. Homework on occasion is only busy work, but optimally it is an additional drill and reinforcer of concepts and skills presented in the classroom. Homework is also an avenue for creative expression and a stimulus for age-appropriate endeavors that stimulate and deepen learning. Grade-school homework assignments commonly involve worksheets of math problems, vocabulary words, sentence completion, spelling words, maps, science or social studies questions. Writing a story or doing a book report is a routine writing assignment. Science, social studies, and history homework may require an elementary form of research, collection of relevant newspaper articles, and accompanying art or chart projects to illuminate the topic of study. Homework is geared to what children can do on their own and is used to deepen knowledge and comprehension. As a tool, homework, teaches responsibility, persistence, and *independent* effort.

Too often, parents become overly embroiled, overly active, and overly anxious; this sets a tone whereby the child feels more and more helpless, fearful that their independent efforts are inadequate; and this causes them to become increasingly dependent on parental help. Hearing accounts of parents laboriously crayoning maps of the thirteen original states, drawing Thanksgiving pictures, and all but writing their child's book reports

suggest they are unable to separate, let go, and enable the
child to be an independent learner. Parents mistakenly
view their child and his or her production as an extension
of themselves, and thereby impose on the child a set of
perfectionistic standards that make it impossible for children to feel confident and secure about their own efforts
and production. Conversely, some parents are too disengaged and aloof and do not cooperate when the child asks
that newspapers be saved, that oatmeal boxes be saved
for an art project. Likewise, some parents are too busy to
look over a child's composition as requested or test them
on spelling words or multiplication tables. A fine balance
of "not too little" and "not too much" help must be
provided to support the child's evolving independence in
the learning process. Parental recognition and praise are
especially necessary in the elementary grades, because
young children initially "work for love." It is only later
that they study and produce because of "love of work"
(Ekstein 1969b).

In elementary school, the child's desire is to please the
parents. Optimally this is soon followed by a wish to
please and form an identification with the teacher. Although parents may be dismayed or amused, they can
take pride in their youngsters' comments that the
"teacher knows best." Such an attitude usually signifies
age-appropriate independence from parents. Older children are less motivated by reward and punishment or
good and bad marks, and more motivated by love of the
work itself. It is a long journey until the rewards of love,
approval, and good marks are replaced by inner motivation and intellectual curiosity. The competitive issues

about college and graduate school admissions further delay this process, and unfortunately only a small number of children pursue knowledge of their chosen field for intrinsic pleasure and unique joy. Some gifted youths are passionate about their chosen area of study and invest time and energy in dance, art, music, science, computers, chess, or other such pursuits.

The average child may not have any such area of special interest. Nevertheless, children's experience of the lower grades sets down enduring study habits and attitudes and approaches to learning and mastery. Success is self-enhancing; struggle and failure create ever-expanding helplessness, poor self-esteem, defensiveness, and more and more barriers to the learning process. Parents can do much to shape their children's responses to the challenges of school work and age-appropriate social relationships. Reasonable order and structure in the home and solid, realistically based praise for good work (not just any production by the child) aid in providing a basis for time management and good standards for appropriate judgment and self-appraisal of work. Agreed-upon study time, realistic limits on television time on school nights, and prioritizing time for work and play are important.

Last but not least is the emphasis on consistent pleasure reading. Library cards and routine library time are important to encourage the young child's curiosity, comfort with written words, and the habit of exploring new topics and new books. If reading is a problem for a child, this should be evaluated as early as possible lest the entire area of reading become contaminated by fear and anxiety.

Working with children who present a range of learning problems suggests that reading problems are the most crippling disorders of all. Major interference in learning is expected when children remain poor readers, unable to synthesize concepts, directions, story lines, or major themes and issues of the history, social studies, or geography text. Poor readers confess to using one book again and again, grade after grade, for book reports, and they share painful accounts of laborious reading without understanding. Any reading difficulty is always apparent in the elementary grades, and prompt consultation with teachers is essential to prevent an unending pattern of pain and poor performance if not addressed. Remedies are numerous and may involve regular parent–child reading sessions, extra school-based help, private tutoring, psychotherapy, and/or school replacement. No appropriate remedy can be selected until a careful assessment of the problem is made. Parents' frustration must not cause them to fail to empathize with the child and to recognize the child's degree of distress.

Assessment of learning problems must be done with the alacrity demonstrated when a child complains of an earache or toothache. Prompt attention supports the child who thereby does not feel alone and increasingly lost in what feels like a sea of quicksand. The many different types of learning disturbances are caused by a myriad of possible emotional, developmental, sociocultural, perceptual, and/or intellectual factors that require study and evaluation to effect remediation. Whatever the cause, a learning disability, when unattended, creates a steady, insidious cumulative trauma similar to other handicaps that cause uneven self-esteem, a sense of help-lessness, and, frequently, rigid defensiveness and inade-quate coping strategies. If ignored, learning disability is more than a school disability; it can become a total life disability. Research suggests that accompanying aca-demic learning problems are frequently based on the lack of cognitive abilities for social skills, such as recognition of social cues, interpretation of nonverbal signals, and understanding nuances in emotional exchanges.

Vignette

Ruth, 9 years old and of Scotch–English Protestant background, was referred for therapy by her mother, a single, full-time employed parent. Ruth is an only child. Her mother had opted for out-of-wedlock single parenthood because of her intense desire for a child. The father lives on the opposite coast, and in accord with the parents' arrangement, he has no pa-ternal or financial responsibility. Contacts between child and father have occurred only twice. Ruth has been informed of the circumstance of her birth; she asks few questions about her father and expresses no longings for attachment or contact. Because financial necessity compels her mother to be continuously em-ployed full time, she returned to her job as a high school teacher after several months of maternity leave and placed Ruth in a good day care center.

Ruth is a bright youngster and upon entrance into elementary school was placed in a class for gifted

children in the public school system of a large urban
community. She is attractive and sturdy in her appearance. Her dark red hair is cut very short, and she has a
gamin look when animated and lively. More commonly she appears somber and depressed and is often
given to silences at school, at home, and in therapy sessions. By contrast, her mother and teacher describe her
as more lively when interacting with peers. The reasons
for referral are her apparent depression, writing disability, and resultant inability to independently handle
her schoolwork or homework. Her mother confessed
to out-of-control sarcasm and angry explosiveness at
Ruth, due to her frustration at her daughter's helplessness, refusal to persevere, and agitated, hysterical demands for endless assistance in completing her
homework. Ruth is a very bright, articulate child, who
possesses unusual perceptiveness. She uses a cryptic
concise style in noting her observations, and most generally she is quiet, depressed, and circumspect. She is
undisciplined and sloppy in her appearance, the care of
her room, and the appearance of her school papers and
homework. Her mother belatedly came to realize that
her permissiveness about such things, in contrast to her
own rigid and demanding upbringing, caused her to
exert little discipline and thus to imply to her daughter
from early on that a sloppy approach was adequate.
Change is now hard to make.

Her mother's forthright honesty, self-appraisal, and
willingness to make changes constituted the backbone
of the therapy effort. Ruth was seemingly too depressed to care and became frightened as her mother

began to disengage from the vicious nightly home-work battles. A tutor was secured for a brief period, and Ruth and the therapist engaged in play therapy sessions in which they played school and examined the anxieties and writing problems that caused Ruth to hold back from trying. Gains began to be reflected in school, management of homework, and after-school sports such as swimming and ice skating as Ruth showed increasing courage to take risks and to do things more independently. A greater degree of confidence enabled Ruth to become more open and out-going in peer interactions. The academic gains paralleled personal growth, overall greater independence, and improved peer relationships. The depression lifted as Ruth felt freer to openly discuss her anger at her mother. Her mother could "take it" and acknowledge Ruth's right to feel angry, given her mother's earlier sarcasm and excessive anger.

Before treatment, Ruth had been apprehensive of directly expressing anger at her mother, the only relative she could depend on. Fearful of rejection and abandonment, she had turned her anger inward and became depressed, inhibited, and too fearful to risk trying lest she do poorly and further alienate her mother. Like many children of teachers, Ruth sees school as a specially loaded area for performance and failure, because it is such a priority to her mother. Without the alliance and support of a father or sibling, Ruth had feared alienating her mother by more direct, assertive expressions. The aggression that had been expressed in covert and passive ways and via depression now became available for positive investment and energetic involvement in sports, academics, and school-based projects such as theater and choir. Learning and mastery require some degree of energy and aggression to tackle tasks and to persevere, and Ruth's aggression now had a positive outlet for age-appropriate mastery in the time of life called the age of industry.

6

Middle School: Puberty—Upheaval and Biological Change

NORMAL DEVELOPMENT AND MATURATIONAL ACHIEVEMENTS OF PUBERTY

Puberty or pre-adolescence is marked by increased separation from the parents and at times the frantic search for new attachments. It is a period of great stress even for model youngsters. The efforts at emotionally separating from parents coincide with the period of diminished coping skills and high vulnerability. The challenge of dealing with all the biological and psychosocial changes is enormous. Normally, parental values and standards have already been embedded in the young person, but during puberty, shifts of varying intensity are made toward emotional separation and independence. The search for new intense attachments in the form of best friends, boy- or girlfriends, or peer groups is an effort to escape loneliness, isolation, and depression. More intellectually directed or artistic youngsters attempt to handle the emotional stress of this period through immersion in creative endeavors (for instance, poetry, music, drama, politics, or academics). Others engage in a hectic athletic program. More impulsive children often demonstrate short-lived, atypical delinquent acts. In the more troubled group there may be involvement in substance abuse, serious delinquency, strange religious affiliations, or fringe activities like cults and secret societies.

In the normal search for new attachments, friends are often overidealized as the parents are defied and denigrated. The peer group becomes the all-important bridge away from the family nest. Uncomfortable sexual feelings and strivings may be played out in actual sexual experimentation, daydreaming, fantasizing, or masturbation. Romantic relationships and best-friendships often exemplify the young adolescent's search for the missing perfection of the self, the ego ideal.

Early adolescent pubescent children face new and dramatic social demands in their roles as teenagers, most commonly in the middle-school or junior-high-school setting that was devised to ease the transition from self-contained classrooms and single teachers of elementary school to rotating classes and multiple teachers of high school (Hamburg 1974). In reality, junior high is rarely a place of gradual transition but in fact duplicates the conditions and multiple transitions of the high-school setting. The academic expectations of middle school involve a sharp, sudden increase in work and achievement pressures. These realities constitute a significant discontinuity with the recent elementary-school experience and the friendship circles of the lower grades. There is a need for peer connections and an uncertainty about one's ability to make new friendships.

The biological changes are considerable, and many specifics of the endocrine changes are now known. No studies reliably relate the hormonal changes of puberty to specific measures of anxiety, hostility, or self-esteem. Nevertheless, observers, especially parents and teachers, concur about, and suffer from, the intensification of moodiness and hostility in the pubescent child.

Early in puberty, pubic hair and ancillary hair appear, boys' voices deepen, and males, behind females in height, commonly evidence a real growth spurt about age 14. Girls begin to show pubertal changes about 2 years earlier than boys. Breast development is the first external manifestation of their beginning sexual maturation and is evident by the age of 10 or 11, well before the appearance of pubic hair. Menarche occurs at about 12½ years, often with initially irregular menstrual cycles.

Children's vastly different rates of maturity create different social consequences for boys and girls. Overall, early maturation has distinct advantages for boys and disadvantages for girls; early-maturing boys are perceived as more masculine, and later-maturing boys who appear childish and slender in build are perceived and treated as less mature and responsible by both adults and peers. Early-maturing boys appear more self-confident and less dependent than their later-developing peers. By contrast, early-maturing girls are often seen as submissive, self-conscious about breast development, and lacking in poise, whereas late-maturing girls are more outgoing, assured, and frequently in positions of leadership in their schools (Hamburg 1974).

Bodily changes that produce anything atypical and highly unusual create a sense of discordance, with resultant self-consciousness, shame, and turmoil. The late-maturing boy is considered the most severely disadvantaged. He continues to look like an elementary school child when it is important for him to be as grown up as possible. He has a developmental lag of about four years as compared to the average girl at the same age and about two years in relation to the age-matched boy (Hamburg 1974). This slow-to-grow male child commonly suffers self-consciousness and low self-esteem and compensates with swaggering bravado, anxiety, and provocative, risk-taking, aggressive behavior. All adolescents, however, struggle with their body image and sense of self, a struggle closely related to the course of physical development. It is important to recognize the pain and inner agony of the pubescent youngster, who must deal with late breast development, severe acne, obesity, awkwardness, and possible physical disfiguration. This is a time of life when looking like one's peers is highly prized, and clothing is often slavishly conforming.

The effects of the biological changes of puberty, including a changed body image, are not the only special tasks to master during early adolescence. Increased academic expectations often make the child apprehensive of inadequacy and failure. Some researchers even suggest that students who experience a prolonged decline in academic performance in junior high are rarely able to improve at a later point in their high-school careers. The key is *prolonged decline,* since most pubescent children experience some dips and unevenness in academic achievement. Grades in elementary school are highly related to intelligence; by contrast, in junior high, motivation seems to be the important factor.

The young adolescent has undergone some changes in style of cognitive functioning, and at this age no longer thinks in rote operational terms but has matured to some use of logic, reasoning, and abstract thinking, although less than the older adolescent. Many still rely on a concrete approach to a greater degree and frequently cannot generalize and transpose concepts. Many, preoccupied with bodily changes and inner concerns, have difficulty concentrating and completing tasks. Rebelliousness and acting-out behaviors are not uncommon in the junior-high-age population. Defiance of adults and compliance with peers are evident in dress codes and in sex, alcohol, and drug experimentation. Educators generally acknowledge that this period of life is characterized by the highest degree of turbulence, unruliness, belligerence, and defiance, all of which greatly interfere with ordered learning and study patterns. Entrance into the teen world is a combination of rebellion toward adults and slavish submission to the peer culture, marked by adherence to styles of hair, clothing, musical tastes, and various other trappings of the youth culture.

THE ROLE OF THE PARENT

Patience, humor, and firmness are required for parents' survival during the upheaval of puberty. Many parents try to cling to the more peaceful latency period in a vain effort to stave off adolescence. Some children will initially comply superficially, but parents soon recognize empty politeness without consideration, conversation without content, and mechanical performance without personal involvement. Resentment and rebellion soon appear in various overt and covert forms, often accompanied by a breakdown in grooming, care of possessions, and capacity to concentrate; frequently some degree of academic decline is apparent.

In the recent past, parenting literature stressed adolescent independence and autonomy, which in fact are more applicable to the older adolescent than to the pubescent youngster. Total freedom is disastrous for the pre-teen or young teenager. At a time of major discontinuity, upheaval, and dramatic bodily change, young adolescents suffer when parental guidance and limit setting are abruptly surrendered. Such freedom may push the youngster toward uncritical acceptance of and attachment to the peer group as a model and major ally. When the peer group is organized around drugs or acting-out behaviors, there is potential for considerable damage and danger (Mishne 1986).

Recent research and writing stress the maintenance of a strong parental coalition against the child's negative choices, wishes, and behaviors. This is easier said than done; parents are vulnerable because they feel dethroned and under constant bombardment by the child's shifting moods, new inaccessibility, and defiance. Parents are bewildered to see frequently declining coping skills, diminished academic performance, and dramatic shifts in choice of friends. When pubescent young teens bombard their parents and themselves with concerns about appearance and social adequacy and with demands for independence, parents ideally must offer their child a response that embodies empathy and firmness. Mothers and fathers have optimally maintained an alliance through effective parenting even in cases of divorce, and such cooperation is especially needed during puberty. When parents are not united or when there is a single-parent household, this period is one of the most difficult to weather. It requires effort and commitment by parents and, at times, support from relatives and extended family members. When parents feel they are losing control, professional help is often required.

Parental humor is not insignificant in the face of adolescents' sudden indifference, projections, aggression, and withdrawal, aptly characterized by the well-known dialogue between child and parent. "Where are you going?" "Out!" "What are you going to do?" "Nothing!" "Who are you going to see?" "No one!" Parents can be comforted by knowing that children at this age turn emotions into opposites, and their angry words and acts should not be taken at face value. Thus love is turned into hatred and respect into contempt, to conceal the hidden but underlying strong bond between the child and themselves. The adolescent does not expect to be taken literally and reacts with confusion to parental helplessness and diminished confidence (Mishne 1986).

In the past, realistic parental anger has not been sufficiently valued as a positive and binding force; more recently it has gained respectability as appropriate and as signifying the relationship between restrictions and limit-setting roles on one hand and nonabandonment on the other. Parental reproaches signify protection and caring. It is important that parents not back down, give up, or manifest exhausted indifference. Most critical is the need to persevere and to keep voices and anger within normal limits. Explosions, physical battles, and excessive punishments are doomed to fail, and commonly induce more rebellion as the child feels entitled to retaliate. Not all things can be resolved by compromise; whatever can be resolved should be attempted when possible, to allow children some space, sense of autonomy, and face saving, to prevent communication from completely breaking down. Parent capitulation, distancing, overindulgence, and attempts to be pals fail to address the struggle for separation and greater age-appropriate independence.

Parents often respond on the basis of the unresolved issues of their own adolescence. For example, parents may try to rebel against a rigid and autocratic upbringing by adopting a totally permissive approach with their children. This approach generally backfires and leads to disastrous and bewildering acting out by children. Effective parenting must be based on firmer ground than simply offering the child the opposite of the parents' own youth. Parents have not traveled the same path as their children; the new realities of drugs, violence in schools and neighborhoods, increased crime, AIDS, and soaring teen pregnancies create a most difficult world for today's youth. Some children and families are at greater than ordinary risk and require more supports and authority than exists in the home. Parents generally wisely recognize what they can and cannot handle independently and, if necessary, seek assistance outside the home by consulting a pediatrician, a member of the clergy, a teacher, or outside child specialists.

Throughout the turbulence and stress, ideally, parental empathy is maintained and the parent is aware of what might be lurking behind ugly and unlovable behavior. Understanding one child's pain must not translate into accepting the unacceptable or covering up or trying to shield the child from the consequences of his or her actions. More troubles will come, if the child is always bailed out by the parents: the same unacceptable behaviors may repeat or worsen. Thus, it is ill advised to try to circumvent the rulings of schools, camps, or even juvenile court. If children are caught stealing, cheating, or drug dealing, the consequences need to be experienced to curtail further infractions. In addition to standing by children as they face the consequences, parents may find it useful to get professional help. Firmness, empathy, and parental cooperation on the youngster's behalf are ideal attributes, which are frequently absent in homes where parents struggle with their own marital, employment, and financial problems. When parental empathy breaks down, a sense of responsibility hopefully will prevail, motivating the parents to seek skilled professional help for both the child and themselves to begin a healing process. The pubescent teenager endures a special inner loneliness despite the seeming hustle and the circle of peers, and it is crucial that he or she feel cared about amid the expected struggles of this age. Abandonment in any form is their greatest fear, and parents must realize they may lose

many battles, but if they demonstrate commitment, they
will win the war.

ESSENTIAL HOME-BASED STRATEGIES TO
SUPPORT SCHOOL ACHIEVEMENT

The pubescent youngster in a traditionally intact home is
buffered in meeting the crisis of early adolescence.
Studies of such families have noted model adolescents in
homes where parents provide stability, empathy, and
consistency (Offer 1967, Offer and Sabshin 1963, Offer
et al. 1965). In such homes the process of detachment
seems less dramatic and less conflicted than traditional
child development theory suggests. These teens are less
submissive to the peer culture and continue to comfortably utilize parental guidelines and the resources and ties
of the nuclear family. The teens studied were from well-
educated, affluent homes where parents were quite sophisticated about child rearing, and parent–child
struggles centered mainly over such minor matters as
dress, style, or music. In these homes, academics were
valued by parents and children, and relatively little new
support was required to help child continue handling
school and social life with the usual zest and motivation
demonstrated earlier. Studies of ideal homes significantly
challenge older concepts of universal and inevitable early
adolescent upheaval, but such model homes and teens are
not in the majority.

More turbulent upheavals undeniably occur in many
families; repudiation of parental values occurs across

class lines, in many lower socioeconomic groups, and in upper-middle-class and intellectual groups (Hamburg 1974). Pressured, overworked parents with little education and economic means tend to be overly strict and often punitive. Especially in homes with absent fathers, the rebellion can be extreme. In many intact and single-parent households among middle-class and intellectual groups, parents are likely to "let go" of their children prematurely to allow autonomy and independence, which in fact is not appropriate until the adolescent is older.

A number of studies have examined parental interest and children's self-esteem. The child's self-confidence is highest and adjustment the best in homes where parents are interested and knowledgeable about the child's friends, activities, and school assignments. All available evidence supports the concept that parental interest makes guidelines fairly easy to maintain, especially when the same-sex parent holds the line on behavioral and academic expectations. It is erroneous to adhere to the old notion of the "generation gap." Rather, "bridging the gap" and manifesting interest in all aspects of the life of the young teen is optimal, to maintain effective communication about school and friends.

Maintaining a distinction between "too much" and "too little," the most favorable situation involves a child living with parents who are interested and involved, but not intrusive, clingy, and overly protective. Discussions are fruitful, and the parents permit realistic choices about friends, time management, homework time, and course of study. The child is permitted some degree of autono-

mous decision making and is allowed space, but not a free
rein. If grades drop and responsibilities are ignored, parental involvement temporarily increases, until the child
presents a steadier course. Parents recognize that they
cannot make the child study, concentrate in class, or
handle homework in a responsible, thorough fashion;
but when problems surface the parent steps in, nonpuni-
tively, in an effort to try to understand the youngster's
worries or preoccupations. Academic difficulty is not
concealed, because the child is secure in the knowledge
that there will be no angry or punitive consequence;
instead, extra help in the form of parental aid or tutoring
will be provided. The parent(s) will not do the work or
become overly embroiled, but will be very interested in
the results of the geometry test and the teacher's assessment of the history research paper. Parents need to value
all school activities and make efforts to attend their
child's athletic events, performances in school plays, and
concerts.

In many instances parents must occupy a more active
and supervisory role to help youngsters manage their
time and work–play priorities. Common limits involve
forbidding television and phone calls until homework is
completed. Clearly the parents cannot sit with or oversee
their child's every movement. Some youngsters covertly
rebel and defy such limits; some storm out of the house
and socialize on school nights; and parents feel helpless
and defeated in the face of their children's proclamations
that there is no homework or that it was completed in
study hall. Such patterns are common in homes where
children's academic achievement is poor and where work

is not a priority or is handled at the most superficial level. Parents cannot lock up their child, but they must create some sort of reward–consequence system. Dialogues such as this can be fruitful:

> I attended Open House at your school, and parents were informed that homework is assigned in at least three subjects nightly. So no matter what you tell me, you couldn't possibly have completed your work with any degree of care or thoroughness. Last marking period you received two deficiencies, and you need to be pulling your grades up. I can't make you do the work, but there will be consequences for lousy grades—long- and short-term consequences. Poor final grades will require summer school attendance to improve your record. In the short run, you should not plan to hold the two parties you mentioned. Life isn't all about play and friends; the choice is yours. We won't reward irresponsible behavior or ignore your disregarding your job. If you need help and are avoiding work that's tough, we'll get you a tutor, but we're not going to go on being ignored. We can schedule a conference and meet with you and your teachers, if we can't rely on you to be accurate in the discussion and proper management of your work.

Vignette

Parents must realize that they can neither overinvolve themselves in their young teens' work nor abdicate all parental responsibility. Their goal is to make children learn independently, and some children take longer than others to reach this goal. Some parents hold on

too tightly and become overinvolved, as in the following example.

Sarah's upper-middle-class Jewish parents had just
transferred her to a private school where work demands were more rigorous than at her previous
school. Sarah responded with an academic decline. Her
papers were rushed and sloppy, and she crammed at
the last minute, wasting time on the telephone and
getting to her work the last thing in the evening. Her
parents became alarmed and overinvolved themselves,
going to the library for her and participating in her
assigned projects to such a degree that Sarah felt increasingly dependent on them. Her procrastination
served to draw them in, and so the pattern persisted.
Speaking with the therapist, the parents insisted that all
the parents at Sarah's school similarly engaged, as they
did, to help their children excel. The father recounted
the same efforts from his own parents, and noted his
subsequent fine high-school grade point average. The
therapist's continued questions revealed, however,
that he had almost flunked out of college in his
freshman year. It took some months of therapy to pry
the parents loose from Sarah's schoolwork and help
them see that she would suffer a fate similar to her
father's unless she was allowed the years of middle and
high school to refine her own study habits and develop
confidence and independence about her schoolwork.

Gradually Sarah's parents withdrew from their participation in their daughter's homework, after excessively helping her compensate for her last-minute
approach to major research projects. They could joke
about the family's immersion in Sarah's Greek studies

project, when the mother had handled Greek food and the preparation of Greek menus and dishes while the father had combed the library to photocopy endless Greek vases and examples of Greek architecture for the art posters he made. Although Sarah wrote the research paper herself, they all slowly realized that the A Sarah received for this project was in fact not earned by her. Receiving a C for a project in middle school might well be the kind of lesson she needed to learn to be motivated to better plan her work schedule. This issue was highlighted by Sarah's final grades, which were lower than previously, and by her not being placed in an advanced math section. These report card realities jolted Sarah, who is a bright youngster. She vowed to change things around; and, the following semester, working *independently,* Sarah raised her grades to B + and A. She also was moved into the prized advanced math class. Her work was handled with more time and care and she stopped dismissing her mother's comments about sloppiness as "Mom's issue" after she saw that she had indeed been marked down for sloppiness by her teachers. Sarah and her parents agreed that television and phone time would follow completion of her homework, and her parents stepped back to allow her to autonomously handle her homework, study, and preparation for all tests.

Vignette

Not all situations were so easily or quickly remedied especially in single-parent households where divorced parents have failed to establish a cooperative parenting alliance and instead are embroiled in ongoing conflict about visitation, child support, and the like. Because of the prevalence of divorce, such a situation is presented here. A child's serious personal and family problems are often displaced onto the school situation and cause major academic decline, truancy, school refusal, non-performance, and failing a grade. Since school is a child's job, the situation can be aptly compared to the job of an adult, whose struggles with personal, economic, and marital problems cause him or her to falter at the job, unable to manage tasks that he or she is well equipped and well educated to handle with competence under ordinary circumstances.

At the age of 11, Chris was referred for therapy by his divorced mother, a woman of middle-class Greek Orthodox background, who was understandably most upset by her son's complaints of severe depression and refusal to go to school at the beginning of each week after visitations with his father. Nightly struggles occurred over homework preparation. Chris frequently panicked and claimed he could not understand or complete his assignments; soon his panic escalated, and Chris more and more often refused to attend school because he had not completed his work and feared reprimands from his teacher. Chris had always been in classes for the gifted, with straight A report cards, and it was clear that serious emotional problems, not lack of intellectual capacity, were causing his troubles. Parents and child were seen by the therapist; the father opted to disengage and refused to cooperate with the mother and the therapist on Chris's behalf. This was not the father's first disengagement. Life-long, father–son contact had been characterized by a pattern of separations and inconsistency. Treatment began on a crisis-intervention basis, given the urgency of Chris's needs, his regression, and his panic states. The immediate goals were to calm child and mother, to diminish the panic, and to stave off the regression inherent in his tantrums, school refusal, and academic difficulty so that he might regain progressive develop-ment. Treatment proceeded effectively and produc-tively, and Chris was able to use his outstanding intellectual and verbal capacities to discuss feelings, thoughts, questions, ideas, and events in his life. He spoke of enjoying his therapy sessions and came ea-gerly. His mother was helped to handle her son more calmly and to lend him emotional support if he re-gressed when feeling overwhelmed by school assign-ments.

Grades improved and a better level of adjustment ensued, but when Chris entered puberty proper, he experienced very sudden bodily changes and an inor-dinate growth spurt. Overnight, it seemed, he towered over his mother, and his unruly behavior now had new dimensions. This time of turbulence unfortunately co-incided with changes in his mother's life, which greatly unsettled Chris. Working at a publishing company that was downsizing and increasing its pressures on staff, his mother was forced to put in extraordinary overtime; she complied from fear of losing her job. This reality resulted in Chris's being on his own too many hours each day. His mother was further distracted by the demands of an important new relationship in her personal life. Chris's gains evaporated, and his old problems resurfaced in more extreme form. Despite the school's recognition of Chris's outstanding intellectual endowment, he could not be promoted that year because of extensive absences and incomplete work. His mother was frequently incapable of getting him out of the house and off to school. Despite solid achievement and grade-appropriate functioning in an overnight summer tutoring school-camp program, Chris faltered when at home and could not perform. Homebound tutoring had to be arranged while Chris resided with grandparents until a boarding-school plan could be arranged.

As is apparent, the problems that became manifest in Chris's school attendance and academic achievement related to personal and family dysfunction and in no way reflected this young boy's intellectual capacities or his school's program. The inability to developmentally handle the psychological, social, and academic tasks of puberty and early adolescence caused breakdown and school failure. Chris's school-based problems were accompanied by home-based and social problems; he became estranged from friends, increasingly defiant and unmanageable at home, impulsive, with bouts of stealing, gorging on food, and wild expenditures of monies. He required a calmer, firmer, and more protected living situation than his single mother could provide, despite her significant efforts and motivation to help her son. Under the strains of single parenting and considerable financial and employment pressures, she could not help but repeat some of the traumatic aspects of her own childhood in attempting to deal with her son. Her therapy enabled her to work through her guilt and move on to secure for her son the best possible out-of-home care.

Such an outcome is not unique or discouraging, if the family can be helped to move ahead and to make suitable arrangements. Chris is young and talented, and prompt procurement of help insures his long-range future. Though all were disappointed that he could not be successfully treated and maintained at home, family commitment to Chris did not waiver. His escalating needs were responded to in a caring and responsible fashion. For children who need a special program, the wide range of possibilities includes therapeutic schools, supervised afterschool programs, day treatment programs, partial hospitalization, boarding schools, and, in extreme cases, hospitalization. Professional consultation and assessment help in the selection of, and referral to, the proper treatment plan or program.

In Chris's case, boarding school proved to be the successful solution. His mother reported that at age 15½ "He's strong and happy now, 6'1" tall and 185 pounds, so his body is under his control. He is doing well in school, A's and B's, is busy with friends and snowboarding four to six times a week. Life is really good. I visit him about twice a month, and as they have school 6 days a week, he has plenty of vacation time for visits home."

7

High School:
Adolescence—
A Normative Crisis

NORMAL DEVELOPMENT AND NATURAL
ACHIEVEMENTS OF ADOLESCENCE

Anna Freud, Sigmund Freud's daughter, was originally a teacher and later trained as a child psychoanalyst. Miss Freud and her former analyst student, Erik Erikson, were the first to focus on the adolescent phase of children's lives. Miss Freud delineated adolescence as a unique and specific period of late childhood characterized by normative upheaval and turmoil. Erikson made a great contribution to our understanding of adolescence as the period that promotes the sense of personal identity. The sociologist Kenneth Keniston noted that adolescence, as understood today, was discovered only in the nineteenth and twentieth centuries. After this period had been acknowledged as significant, contemporary society began to support this phase of development by providing educational, economic, institutional, and familial resources for teenagers (Mishne 1986). While there have been some recent challenges to the traditional views of the extent of normal turmoil and upheaval, there is complete agreement on the special needs of this age group. These needs include resources for creativity, recreation, and advanced academic study. Most important are role models with whom to identify. Those lacking admirable role models close at hand, such as parents, teachers, relatives, and so on, too often attach to unattainable figures of fame in the sports and entertainment fields, for instance, rock stars, movie stars, models, and athletes, who attract cultlike mass followers from the adolescent population.

Miss Freud's classic description of the normal disharmony of adolescence elegantly portrays the baffling contradictions of the teenager.

> I take it that it is normal for an adolescent to behave for a considerable length of time in an inconsistent and unpredictable manner; to fight his impulses and to accept them; to ward them off successfully and to be over-run by them; to love his parents and to hate them; to revolt against them and to be dependent on them; and be deeply ashamed to acknowledge his mother before others and, unexpectedly, to desire heart-to-heart talks with her; to thrive on imitation of and identification with others, while searching unceasingly for his own identity; to be more idealistic, artistic, generous and unselfish than he will ever be again, but also the opposite, self-centered, egotistic, calculating. Such fluctuations between extreme opposites would be deemed highly abnormal at any other time of life. [Freud 1958, p. 275]

In contrast to this longstanding traditional view about the inevitability—in fact, the desirability—of turbulence during adolescence, a number of researchers have suggested that the extreme upset of adolescence is not universal and inevitable; that the personality upheaval of this phase of life can be reflected primarily in manageable, nondebilitating rebellion, a depression, and minor acting-out behaviors. A number of contemporary researchers (Douvan and Adelson 1966, Offer et al. 1965, Oldham 1978, and Rutter et al. 1976) state that adolescents normally maintain psychic equilibrium while struggling with developmental tasks; and that they are usually able to make successful adjustments in their social and family relationships, while having only minor disagreements with authority figures.

"Adolescence proper" (ages 14 to 17) is characterized by an intense emotional life, a turning toward romantic attachments, and an increased detachment from parents. This age-appropriate push for more independence than earlier is not a happy or easy course; most teens experience some degree of pain, depression, and fear at the prospect of having to be less dependent and more separate from parents. Some writers have likened adolescence to stages of mourning and being in love. Renouncing one's parents as one's salvation and base of security causes inner emptiness, grief, and sadness, which is part of all mourning (Blos 1962). Withdrawal from the parents stimulates greater self-absorption and self-preoccupation. The teenager is actually struggling to seek and find new love connections to replace the surrendered parents, and this process commonly creates moodiness, belligerence at home, and exaggerated assessments of his or her strengths and capabilities. With the increasing estrangement from parents, many teenagers overvalue the peer group and special friends or romantic partners. The arrogance and grandiosity of the adolescent creates rebellion and increased defiance of the parents' authority. Parental approval is of less importance than peer approval, and daydreams or fantasies of inordinate power and success often occupy the teenager. Friendships are made and broken, and the frantic search goes on as the adolescent struggles for meaning, direction, and close emotional ties.

The self-absorption and sense of entitlement promote an intimate sense of self, whereby the child becomes increasingly aware of sexual arousal, anger, and tension. There is a longing for, and fear of, closeness and trust, along with strict conformity to the chosen youth group or subgroup. This excessive attachment to the peer group helps ward off a sense of loneliness and personal insecurity. Choice of peers is critical and may be positive or negative, depending on the adolescent's own self-image. Some align with successful athletes and students; others, with friends of artistic, musical, and literary interests. Politics beckons still others, and many, unfortunately, move toward peers exhibiting acting-out behaviors such as risk-taking experiments with sex, drugs, and alcohol. The most at-risk teens are loners, estranged youths, and those affiliated with violence-prone gangs. Peer groups and gangs are commonly referred to as families: many youths are too fearful to be genuinely independent.

Cognition normally becomes more realistic, objective,

and analytic, and more advanced academic work is handled. Rote learning is replaced by logic, reasoning, and
the ability to transpose knowledge from one situation to
the next. School assignments no longer pursue pure facts.
Essays and reports are now expected to demonstrate
comprehension of abstract matters like emotions, mo-
tives, group processes, belief systems, and interpersonal
ways of relating. At this age, specific interests, skills, and
talents have emerged and the older adolescent, close to
graduation from high school, normally has more stable
self-esteem. Vocational choices are being weighed and
sorted out realistically as high school academic choices
are made, for example, about which foreign language to
study and which colleges to consider. Self-appraisal by
middle- and upper-middle-class adolescents commonly
is heavily reliant on their level of academic success and
their status in the peer group. As the planning for college
unfolds, friends and their college choices, as well as one's
own grade point average (GPA), take on increased meaning. College is the goal of an expanding segment of
society: first-generation college applicants with limited
financial resources examine local and junior colleges and
work–study programs. Departure from high school is
longed for and feared as teenagers face expectations for
more autonomous functioning. The job market for high
school graduates is rather dismal: those who lack solid
technical skills or vocational training are faced with poor
prospects for anything better than a minimum-wage job
with little challenge or future. The non-college-bound
youth optimally has attained vocational skills in mechan-

ics, plumbing, computers, and the like. Currently many college-bound youth appropriate worry about the future job market.

THE ROLE OF PARENTS

As children mature, parents must accommodate by adapting to their youngsters' age-appropriate desire for greater independence. This adaptation requires a flexible stance and an appropriate balance of neither too much nor too little freedom. Teenagers still very much need parental supports, guidance, and limits, despite their belligerent demands to be left alone. If parents capitulate and withdraw from providing supervision and structure, there can be disastrous results. Fifteen- and sixteen-year-olds still require supervision about activities, choices, and curfews. Although implementation is often taxing, such limit setting is appropriately perceived as concern. Teens who can stay out all night do not relish such freedom but rather feel ignored and uncared for. Despite protestations and accounts of what everyone else is allowed to do, adolescents expect and need restraints and consequences if they stay out too late, are irresponsible with the family car, get drunk, suspended from school, and the like.

Ideally, the parent nurtures and supports the independent strivings in ways that are realistic. This means that the course is not characterized by pursuit of the pleasure principle but, rather, the reality principle. Reality requires a focus on work, love, and play, and a proper balance is necessary to equip the adolescent to make appropriate independent choices about handling school, seeing friends, and pursuing recreation. Parents cannot force a teenager to study and succeed in school or hold a job, but they can provide realistic consequences. There is no basis for expecting good judgment from adolescents if they are failing academic courses and having conflicts with teachers. Thus, parents are ill advised to turn the other cheek or to provide the usual privileges, such as ample allowance, lenient curfew, and use of the car, when their children are nonfunctional at school—in essence, at their "job." The job comes first, and good judgment and control must be apparent before parents can realistically trust their adolescent to show good judgment, for instance, behind the wheel of a car. Some teens need limits about allowance, curfew, and acceptable social settings. Ideally, limits are coupled with firm parental discussion and clear expectations. Tightening the rein often suffices, and if not, more parental efforts must be taken. Unrelenting rebellion often is a sign that professional help is needed. It is very hard to hold the line in the face of belligerence, anger, threats, provocations, or calculating maneuvers of teens who can cajole their parents into submission.

In some families there is a constant pattern of "fight and flight," with parents made anxious by angry exchanges which are followed by their youngster's stalking out, or sulking in rageful silence in his or her room. Here again, the parent should not capitulate or surrender to what is, in fact, an adolescent version of a toddler's temper tantrum. Staying calm and clearheaded is easier said than done under the barrage of attack, but calmness and a refusal to accept the unacceptable are necessary.

Compromise and careful consideration are essential when possible, but compromise is not always realistic. For example, (1) "You must be joking if you think I'm going on that youth hostel trip. Bill's and Tom's parents are letting them go cross-country hitchhiking, and I'm going with them!" (2) "Big deal—so what if the teacher thinks I'm stoned and dealing pot! What if I am? Everyone else does too and you can't stop me! If you weren't so cheap and I had an allowance like everyone else, I might not have to do my dealing. You both are stingy and I don't have what I want, like clothes that are cool, and unlimited use of the car." (3) Sally was brought home in a police car after attending a friend's party where two hundred drunken kids ransacked a house in the absence of parental supervision. Sally was picked up for drunken driving after having led the police on a chase as they followed her careening, speeding car. These three examples of dangerous illegal behaviors and risk taking are clearly situations in which no compromise is appropriate or warranted.

Many other situations are not so clear-cut; other situations are created by excessive parental restraints. Some parents attempt overcontrol and attempt to exert excessive restraints on their children's choice of friends and social plans, or have perfectionistic goals regarding academic achievement. Some overburdened parents overburden their adolescents with unrealistic expectations that they assume too much housework and too many child-care responsibilities. In all the variations of parenting patterns, the key is balance, empathy, and the attempt to maintain communication despite anger. Such results can usually be achieved after time out, which lets each party cool off and regain self-composure. Harmony between the parents enables them to maintain a united front or coalition. When this coalition is missing, children may become scapegoats or captives in the triangle of child–mother–father. In such cases a parent–child alliance leaves out one parent. This commonly becomes a destructive cycle filled with animosity and guilt, because adolescents, even when "winning," will feel they are the source of the parent's conflict and estrangement.

Empathy, creativity, wisdom, humor, and the recognition that adolescence is not permanent all are essential in parenting teenagers. At this age "parents have the greatest need for flexibility and strength in reviewing and expanding those enduring values and goals which are basic to a sense of continuity of the self . . ." (Elson 1984, pp. 310 and 311). Parenthood, like child development, is viewed as passing through developmental phases, and none are more difficult than puberty and adolescence proper, when a child feels "superior to their parents and makes no secret of it. The love and affection between the generations which is so clearly present seems also to be continuously in a state of flux" (Offer 1984, pp. xiii and xiv). It is critical to be prepared to live with adolescents' ambivalence and to stay calm in the face of exaggerated views, frequent hostile words, and the resultant anger they can evoke. There is real distinction between loving and liking one's child, and at this age, beloved children often become unlikable for a time. Struggles over manners, choice of friends, cleanliness, secretiveness, hours, and dress are common. Schoolwork looms large in the list of battlegrounds.

Minor breaks in empathy are expected and normal in parenting; indeed they are essential in helping the child develop the personality strength to regulate anxiety (Elson 1984). Parents and children both suffer frustration and disillusionment in the maturation process. Mutual disappointment is necessary in the process of letting go, which enables children to surrender youthful idealization of the parents and the dependency of younger years. Parents must accept the limits of what they can and cannot control and must allow their child the space for more independence and for learning from their own mistakes. The leavening of humor may help parents accept a less central position in their children's lives. Adolescents frequently come to experience an emerging and deepening empathic awareness of what their parents went through during adolescence, and what they themselves put their parents through on their own road to maturity. "One can only attempt to weather anxiety and fears and affirm and guide one's adolescent but without the confining closeness of the younger years" (Elson 1984, p. 311).

ESSENTIAL HOME-BASED STRATEGIES TO SUPPORT SCHOOL ACHIEVEMENT

By the time of adolescence proper, patterns of study and work habits, level of academic achievement, and social-

ization characteristics are in place. Interests and preferences are becoming increasingly well defined. Change is
possible and does occur; it commonly relates to adolescents' increased motivation now that grades and their
academic record *counts* for college admission. A slump in
middle school can be followed by a major shift and
improvement in achievement, although some studies
have shown that after a real drop in performance in junior
high, it is the rare student who is able to substantially and
spontaneously improve. Professional help may be required for significant change.

When grades are lower than intelligence tests suggest
they can be, it is generally because teens' motivation has
been focused on body image, role change, and relations
with peers, all of which have overshadowed academic
concern. In some instances personal and family emotional problems cause major interference in performance.

The long-range goal of college admission motivates
many adolescents, but generally only if they are in a peer
culture and a school environment that value college and
admission to rigorous programs. James A. Kagan (1971)
observed that young people "are finding it increasingly
difficult to rationalize working for grades." The incentive to use their education as a passport to higher status
and financial security has been somewhat eroded, and
academic achievement is thus meaningless to many.
Many are more fixated on momentary concerns that
cause them to focus almost exclusively on peer-group
status and body image. Placement in optimal school
settings is thus a key to motivation for academic performance. This reality is one of the major explanations for

flights to suburban school districts, as parents struggle to obtain the best possible public education. More affluent parents opt for parochial schools, private day schools, and boarding schools, particularly if they are residents of urban communities whose high schools are generally substandard, with overcrowding, violence, deteriorated physical plants, and negatively oriented peer groups. Because of the central role of the peer group, the selection of school setting is of particular importance during adolescence proper. The selection on occasion can be determined by variables other than family income. Qualified or talented students are awarded scholarships at the high-school level, though competition is fierce, especially during economic recessions when private settings have less monies available. The scholarship awarded does not always remedy the situation: scholarship students endure special and unique pressures, which can produce their own problems.

Vignette

Erica was attending a prestigious private school on scholarship. She was unhappy because she felt alienated from her peer group. Erica had always been an outstanding student, who tested in the superior range. Despite her obvious abilities, her grades were declining although her achievement was still high. She was referred for therapy by her single mother, a hard-working, middle-aged Jewish elementary-school teacher, who had struggled with her meager income since the death of Erica's father. The parents had been divorced, and the father had paid child support. But following his death and the curtailment of his contributions, economic pressures were considerable. Mother and child lived in a lower-class urban community; the mother wanted the best education possible for her talented child, and thereby sought and obtained admission and scholarship assistance at a choice private school where Erica felt estranged from her classmates. Though most attractive, with blonde curly hair and blue eyes, Erica felt and looked depressed; she was ill-kept and described struggles with her weight and bouts of binge eating. She said that she had no pleasure or sense of satisfaction about her schoolwork. She worked erratically, in spurts; at the last minute she crammed for tests and never felt secure, prepared, or pleased with what she produced. Her school advisor had tried to be supportive when they talked, and because she had discussed transferring, the school increased her scholarship in an effort to retain this able student. Erica felt torn because she wanted to leave her school, but she feared disappointing her mother who was so invested in her daughter's school achievement and placement in the special setting.

Erica based her alienation from her peers on economics; she was the poorest child in her school. She poignantly described the shock and scorn her seventh-grade classmates registered when they came to her shabby apartment for a birthday party. Because she had attended birthday parties in their affluent homes, she was keenly aware of the differences. These economic differences were evident in accounts of family vacations over school break, and Erica angrily spoke of snobs taken skiing, to the Caribbean, and the like. She said that after classmates had visited in her home, all invitations to her ceased abruptly. In sum, Erica felt that although her school provided her good teachers and a challenging curriculum, she could not continue to endure the social estrangement. She recognized that her shame and self-consciousness might have contributed to her loneliness and caused her to push peers away, but she also felt the group devalued and mocked her and treated her as different and unimportant. Therapy efforts focused on helping her with her feelings of low self-esteem and on considering alternatives for educational placement. Given her academic aspirations and reluctance to surrender her sense of ownership of her daughter, her mother resisted change. A compromise was worked out when Erica was admitted to a prestigious and competitive special public high school for gifted adolescents. Erica felt at ease and comfortable with this student body because "they're more like me, good students who are college bound, from working-class homes."

Erica's dilemma is not unique. Adolescents cannot easily tolerate being very different from their peer group; although her mother's efforts and aspirations were laudable and understandable, the original school placement was doomed to fail because Erica was excluded from the decision-making process. Such unhappy situations are not infrequent; for instance, a minute number of talented

and bright children of color in otherwise white prestigious public or private schools often experience alienation, loneliness, and consequent academic decline. Thus,
a critical parental strategy is finding the best educational
site and making an assessment that does not overempha-
size academics at the expense of social life and peer
relationships. The final decision must be a mutual one,
involving the high-school student and the parents. In-
vestigating and visiting various schools are in order, to
avoid emotionally and financially costly mistakes, as
when struggling parents stretch themselves to purchase a
new home near a good school, only to find that their
adolescent is the only African American or Latino in the
entire high school.

In addition to choice of setting or community, for
typical public school enrollment the parents should try to
create an atmosphere in the home that values their adolescent's "job" or school performance, but which does
not intrude or hold out perfectionistic goals. Ownership
of the work must be the adolescent's. Excessive parental
involvement is always a contaminate, and interferes with
the child's sense of competence and confidence; problems
will surface at some point in the present, causing exam
anxiety, or in the immediate future, as is the case when
"freshman college panic" undoes many older adolescents. Parents mistakenly think they are helping their
children when they become actively engaged in their
adolescents' schoolwork, typing and correcting their papers, directing research projects, reading their texts so as
to knowledgeably direct them in preparation for exams.

The parental task is to stimulate independence, time

management, intellectual curiosity, and a love of learning. These characteristics are more critical for later life
achievement than a precise grade point average (GPA).
Parents who are overly fixated on the GPA may uninten-
tionally send the wrong message, which is that the teacher's assessment is more important than real love of
learning. Such parental anxiety can discourage intellectual curiosity and related independent reading in favor of
rigid focus on the assignment at hand. Therapists often
hear tales of inordinate parental pressures and anxiety;
for example, commands to "stop reading about Napo-
leon. You're supposed to do a paper on the Civil War!" A
B on the Civil War paper and independent reading and
pursuit of knowledge may better prepare a historian than
simply focusing on the immediate assignment at hand.
High school and college are times for intellectual curiosity and creativity, not simply achievement. Parental
intrusion and demands for the highest level of achievement can kill a love of learning. Parental standards can
undermine adolescents' beliefs in their own capabilities.
For example, a law student who has always relied on his
mother when doing papers still comes home from law
school to work on papers with her. She takes over his
research efforts and the editing and typing of all of his
assignments. One can only wonder what will happen to
this vulnerable young man when he begins to practice
law and obviously cannot take his mother to the office to
help him do research and prepare briefs!

Parental overinvolvement is most common when adolescents underachieve academically. Anger and nagging
are classic examples of parents' vain efforts to prod chil-

dren to work and perform. Many parents alternate between nagging and becoming overly engrossed in the work; they rush out to purchase Cliff Notes, engage in the literal writing of papers, peruse the library for appropriate research sources, and so on.

Teenagers with a history of academic difficulty have developed an image of themselves as failures. They demonstrate incomplete educational experiences and gaps in skill, knowledge, and understanding. Many have limited means of expression, and their creative impulses are blocked or exhibited as negative and hostile acts. By high school age, poor achievers have actively or passively withdrawn from academic involvement, and the withdrawal can be social as well. Many have ceased to attempt new experiences and have rejected the challenge of growing. Generally, they avoid responsibility, demonstrate difficulty in acknowledging feelings, and are insensitive to their impact on others. Because of their constriction and lack of success, they have longstanding low self-esteem. Confidence in their abilities has eroded, and adults and peers are viewed as unreliable (Mishne 1987/1988).

Their parents similarly have often become overwhelmed with shame and a sense of helplessness to effect change. Rage at their adolescent (for putting them in such a position) and at the school (for their child's poor grades) creates a morass. Parents and child need a respite from unproductive patterns around school issues and a relief from eternal feelings of guilt and disappointment. If academic underachievement is of considerable duration and not responsive to ordinary discussions and parental

supports, such as expectations that the adolescent is at
home to study on all school nights, professional intervention is in order. An assessment is a first step in sorting
out the best course, which may be tutoring, therapy, a
combination of both, or replacement in a different
school.

The high-school student should be an independent
learner; excessive involvement of parents in homework
only produces negative effects. Home is where we remain most infantile, and parental involvement in homework is seen as prolonging infantile dependency.
Independent study like homework calls for mature efforts; this effort and its result must become the basis of a
transaction between students and their teachers. If there
are no cognitive, perceptual, developmental, or intellectual problems, academic underachievement is generally
based on problematic parent–child ties and excessive
enmeshment. This excessive closeness is commonly related to family-based transactions created by marital
problems or atypical parental anxiety that infects children. Parents of high-school students *cannot* be agents for
change. Instead, appropriate help should be secured from
objective, skilled professionals. Some schools cannot
easily serve the underachiever because they rely only on
stigmatizing placements in special classes. With the
abundant disruption commonly created by angry and
impulsive underachievers, teachers struggle between efforts to teach and to discipline; positive student–teacher
relationships are rare in such classes. Underachieving
students generally profit from personal or family therapy
and placement in small educational sites with a high ratio

of adults to children and with emphasis on close student–
teacher relationships and communication. Such special
therapeutic schools can provide a place to begin again.
Ideally, competence, creativity, growth, and hope develop. Such special settings are *not* always beyond the
reach of families with limited financial resources. Many
are attached to social agencies, mental health clinics, and
hospitals where fees are scaled according to family income. Specialists in clinical work with children and adolescents offer services beyond assessment and treatment.
They know community resources and frequently act as
referral sources, seeking the right fit between children,
parents, and school setting.

Academic achievement has been much emphasized.
Social competence and comfort, however, are of critical
importance, as was illustrated in the vignette about Erica.
Some good students are also loners or forever on the
periphery of the peer group. Parental efforts should be
directed toward sensitive awareness of adolescents' social
adjustment. Here again, by the time that adolescents are
in high school, parents can do little to directly enhance
their children's social adjustment. Ideally, they have welcomed their children's peers into their home and expressed appropriate interest in their child's friends, and
social, athletic, and recreational activities. When adolescents are isolated and estranged, however, parents cannot
effect change. A quiet, nontroublesome situation sometimes gets overlooked; but if it continues, it can cause
separation problems when college is the next step. Entrance into college and success away from home can be
problematic for such adolescents: they may require

therapy and more time at home before a departure can be successful. The uneven growth rate of youth is such that age-appropriate tasks are often handled on very different timetables. Recognition of and accommodation to the uneven development of adolescents are crucial for their future mastery and success. Some intellectually able adolescents can do fine academic work but not function comfortably away from home at the age of 18, and they may need to wait before leaving home for college. Flexible, individualized accommodation to children's intellectual, social, sexual, and psychological development is necessary to facilitate their genuine entry into comfortable, confident adulthood.

8

College: Late Adolescence and Early Adulthood— Consolidation and Stabilization

Late adolescence is viewed as a stage of consolidation and stabilization. We anticipate and expect clarity and purposeful actions, predictability, steady and enduring emotional balance, steadfast self-esteem, and more mature functioning. The narcissism and self-absorption of earlier adolescence have diminished, and there is a greater tolerance for frustration and compromise (Mishne 1986). The developmental task of normal late adolescence is the consolidation of personality to facilitate stability in handling work, study, love relationships, and personal value systems. The surrender of earlier self-absorption facilitates the move toward the external world, as a source of pleasure and mastery. This is the age of a final and irreversible resolution of the sexual and personal sense of identity. The self is recognized in relation to others, and this is basic to the achievement of a sense of genuine identity. The central issues at this time of life are modulation of impulses and resolution of: acceptance versus rebellion against authority; reconciliation of positive and negative feelings toward the parents; and balancing independent and dependent strivings with idealism and self-interest (A. Freud 1958).

The successful completion of these age-appropriate achievements creates greater stability and clarity in the emotional and intellectual life of older adolescents. There is a newly acquired solidity of character and personal ideals and values. Looking outward, many surrender the earlier self-absorption manifest in creative expression and imagination. Often private poems and songs written in earlier adolescence wane in value and importance. Roles and occupational goals have been selected with a more realistic appraisal of one's strengths and weaknesses. Familial, cultural, and social values become better integrated with one's own ideals and aspirations. Some older adolescents go through some mourning and depression in letting go of earlier hopes and desires as they mature and more realistically accept what is possible. They grow more comfortable living with uncertainty and partially attainable goals. Earlier dreams of glory have been "transformed into the life of feasible possibility" (Kaplan 1984, p. 20).

In late adolescence there is an increased capacity for abstract thought, as well as organized application of intelligence. New tasks, interests, and goals are assimilated by healthy young adults. Romantic ties become more enduring, and stable, and lengthy relationships are formed. The peer group is surrendered as the all-important frame of reference. Group affiliations become secondary to romantic attachment, which is generally accompanied by a return to closer familial ties. Parents and siblings take on a renewed significance, and family relationships are characterized by nondependent affection and more open sharing of confidences and friendship. The renewed parent–young-adult-child tie involves a kind of final surrender of earlier dependency on parents and is characterized by bidding "farewell to childhood" (Laufer 1966). Recently developmental theorists have questioned classic notions of separation and individuation of children from parents at the time that older adolescents move into more autonomous functioning. These clinicians and researchers believe that such concepts fail to define the essence of the human condition; they maintain that people never outgrow the need for parental support, understanding, and admiration. What is outgrown is exploitation and self-absorption that ignore the parents' needs. Thus, parent and young adult relationships ideally become mutually enhancing and supportive (Basch 1983, Elson 1986, Kohut 1971, 1972, 1977, 1984, Stern 1985). The task of young adulthood in relation to parents and others is to achieve mature empathy. As the parents no longer are central, there is a push toward significant relatedness with friends, lovers, employers, and professors. Mature relationships are characterized by union, intimate togetherness, and attunement to the feelings and needs of others.

A final and major task of late adolescence and young adulthood involves commitments to vocation and the work role. Vocational choice is an extremely pressing concern in the 1990s, as reports increasingly document college graduates' inability to find desired positions in their chosen field(s) and their resorting to income-generating labor in lesser positions. Unquestionably, American youths have been profoundly affected by the cultural and societal influences of cycles of affluence, recession, lengthy education and accompanying prolonged financial dependence on parents. The pill, the sexual revolution, drugs, new phenomena like AIDS, the complexity of technology, and the need for extensive training for employment in our accelerated society all increase apprehension about entering the adult world. Some authors have suggested that "the social environment today may indeed be imposing unbearable burdens on the more vulnerable members of this generation" (Holzman 1980, p. 314). Diminished quality education, high unemployment, particularly for minority groups, exposure to violence via the media, and interruption of attachments by divorce, all contribute to young adults' common feelings of apprehension and some degree of hopelessness. The new freedom in personal relationships has created for many an atmosphere of superficiality, transience, and impermanence, creating sadness and depression in many young people.

Current social conditions complicate an important young-adult achievement, that of the formation of a satisfactory philosophy of life and a personally acceptable code of behavior. This relaxation of values and direction entails experimentation and choice during the journey toward acceptance of the self. Self-acceptance and self-respect "carries with it the idea that many emotions, deficits and mistakes of behavior can be tolerated, if not

condoned, along with one's talents, accomplishments
and triumphs" (Arnstein 1984, p. 140).

THE ROLE OF THE PARENT

The rapid social and economic changes characteristic of
contemporary society impact on parents, especially those
with diminished child care responsibilities. Many families are, or become, two-career households, when children are older and no longer in need of the extensive
coverage of the earlier years. There are frequent conflicting expectations between the demands of family and
work, especially for women in the workplace. At the
point when children are off to college, some parents may
not be quite as unburdened as anticipated because aging
parents commonly require added time and attention, a
situation leading to role strain, conflict, and overload for
the "generation in the middle" (Hagestad 1981, Neugarten 1979). Nevertheless, at this time, both parents—
particularly mothers—find themselves increasingly with
free time, since the phase of active parenting generally
comes to an end when children reach mid- to-late adolescence. "Letting go" is a critical task for parents as
offspring leave home to enter college. Those youth who
are not college bound often must remain at home because
of the limitations of their earnings; they need the necessary space for age-appropriate, less dependent functioning. Contrary to earlier notions about parents' depressed
responses to the "empty nest," more recent studies find

that this period is rarely a crisis, especially for fathers—
who then, to a greater degree than mothers, may move
into enjoyment of greater freedom. Failure of young
adult children to leave home at the expected or anticipated time creates increased strain and conflict among
parents and their young adult children, far surpassing any
problems in response to the empty nest. Normally when
children begin to leave home part time for college, they
live more independently but still are part of an interde-
pendent family unit. Frequent personal and telephone
contact is the norm, and vacations at home characterize
parent–child contacts during the college years.

The parents' role at this stage is usually vastly diminished. They provide financial and emotional support but
function at greater distance. Some strain and stress ema-
nate from having to relinquish their earlier, more central
position in their children's lives. In addition, parents are
frequently faced with their young adult children's different standards and beliefs as well as vocational and
romantic choices that may not conform to parents' expectations. Compromise and acceptance of these choices
are frequently necessary to maintain continuity and positive contact. Parents "must endure the sadness their
child's growing up entails, but they may also find creative outlets for the energy formerly absorbed in the task
of child rearing. Even parents who have balanced a full-
time profession and parenthood face this change" (Elson
1986, p. 18).

Parents of young adults worry and struggle with their
own empathic response as they watch their children face
complex changes and disappointments in vocational

opportunities, the newer forms of courtship, and delayed marriages in today's world. Ideally the parent develops an informed and responsive capacity to accept the initiative and perceptions of their children as peers. Parents hopefully have learned the limits of what is possible in relation to their children, whereby they can temper any disappointments and come to as positive a rapport as possible with them. Their trust and belief in their child's capacities serves as a support as the young adult struggles with today's social and economic vicissitudes.

STRATEGIES TO SUPPORT SUCCESS
IN COLLEGE

Parents' actions in supporting their older child's school success differ greatly from their support in the earlier years, when the child resided at home. College-age older adolescents–young adults are more or less "out there" on their own. Nevertheless, family influences continue in the form of parental expectations, attitudes, and values. Many young people enter college easily and make social and academic adjustments with a minimum of discomfort. A sizeable number, however, experience anxiety and apprehension especially in their freshman year. Such reactions occur among students at rigorous and demanding schools, where the nation's valedictorians face more competition than they ever before experienced. Such an experience can unsettle the most able of students. Fierce competition for graduate programs in medicine, law, and psychology cause many students extreme anxiety because of the all-important grade point average (GPA) required for admission. Exam anxiety and performance anxiety are frequent phenomena in the normal college population. Extremely high tuition fees and parental sacrifice to cover school expenses are other sources of anxiety for ambitious students. Thus, academic challenges and pressures are considerable during this developmental milestone marking greater maturity. Equally daunting are social pressures inherent in entering an institution unknown and alone and in adjusting to dormitory life.

Students' response and choices run the gamut and determine parental reactions. Some students settle in and are seriously dedicated to succeeding at the tasks at hand. They study and, slowly and carefully, begin to form friendships and enter into extracurricular sports and other activities. Others, often those feeling relief at their release from excessive parental pressures during high school, sow their oats and behave almost hedonistically at the new freedoms and opportunities. This group may act recklessly and excessively, drinking, partying, and experimenting with sexual promiscuity, alcohol, and drugs. This extreme activity often masks depression and fear of independent functioning. The separation from home may be harder than anticipated, and at all costs, defenses must be maintained against homesickness and anxiety. Males' macho behaviors and girls' excessive partying and drinking commonly are masks for insecurity and fear. Parental anger and threats are generally counterproductive. Far more successful are parental empathy and perception of what lurks behind this maladaptive behavior. This is easier said than done: parents feel anxiety, frustration, and deep disappointment at their children's acting out and irresponsibility. Because many students' underlying anxieties are repressed, they are hard put to explain their actions; instead they respond defensively to parental admonishments. Their overt expressions of independence are not genuine. In fact, their behavior screams out for limits, and behavior speaks louder than words. Rather than functioning more autonomously, students are tightening the parent–child tie via anxiety and worry, thus binding themselves and their parents in a struggle for control. Issues of earlier adolescence are evident in students' slavish conformity to a subgroup of peers versus parental expectation and age-appropriate assumption of responsibility. There is a limit to what restraints can be applied. Some parents take back the student's car in response to drunken behavior; others indicate that change must be made and grades must improve if the student wishes to return to school the next semester or second year.

Parents need to recognize that there is a frequent discrepancy between chronological and emotional age, and thus no lock-step set of rigid expectations can suffice. Some 17- and 18-year-olds are genuinely ready for college and independent living, and others are not. Some flunk out after one semester, and others master the separation and anxiety and settle in, with growing confidence and increasing social and academic success. Some only marginally complete the initial semester(s) and then rather spontaneously move into more competent functioning in the sophomore year. In many situations, a

marginal GPA and academic probation are warnings or
red flags suggestive of more trouble ahead. In such cases,
parents and young adult children have to decide about
the best course to follow. The alternatives are many,
including taking a year off to return home to work;
returning home to enroll in a local college full or part
time; or some combination of the above, accompanied by
seeking psychotherapy. In many situations poor academic performance is concealed until the semester's final
grades reveal the truth. Social difficulties are often more
easily shared: parents recount their misery and helplessness in response to endless calls from their children, who
weep and complain about loneliness and troubles with
roommates. In families where open communication exists, students share their panic and terror about the academic work and pressure and in this way turn to the
parents for help.

Vignette

Bill was desperate after the first weeks at college.
During the weekly, then increasingly frequent, long-
distance calls to his parents, he shared his sense of panic
and terror at not handling his academic work. His
impulsive threats of dropping out increased as he recounted very low marks on initial quizzes and tests.
Long-distance parenting from the west coast posed
great challenges, and the parents recognized they could
do little to comfort or calm their son. After making
inquiries, they referred Bill to a therapist in the city in

which he was studying. Bill accepted the referral eagerly. Having an ally at hand brought some immediate relief; Bill punctually attended his sessions, demonstrating motivation and a desire to master his situation. He was provided emotional support and advised to seek tutoring help and arrange conferences with his professors promptly, lest things escalate to unmanageable proportions.

Bill is a bright, tall, dark, Jewish 18-year-old who did very well the last half of high school. However, his entrance into high school had been marked by the same fears and poor performance apparent when he began college. This repetition is common: the demands for more autonomous functioning in high school constitute a real challenge, especially for those youth who are insecure and vulnerable. Bill's challenges during his first semester of college caused his old anxieties to reverberate.

The conclusion of Bill's first freshman semester proved to be an academic success. He received two Bs and two As and could evidence pride and relief at his accomplishments. He recognized his need to continue in therapy to solidify the gains in academic functioning and to get to the underlying sense of insecurity that repeatedly caused his problems. He was aware of his lifelong competition and sense of inadequacy compared to his older, successful sister, who "did well without even trying." Despite parental assurances, he nevertheless deeply believed his father wanted him to follow in his footsteps and be a corporate lawyer, and so he had opted to take political science and economics in the hope that he would do well enough to be able to make that career choice if he later decided. Bill noted his irrational guilt over his preferences for art history and philosophy. "Things that lead to no secure career are what interest me most. I can't tell you how much my philosophy course excites me. We read great stuff, and the professor is the best."

Bill was aware of his social struggles, and although he felt more at ease with males and more able to connect and make friends, he was reticent with girls. He had kept his girlfriend from high school, due to fears of college dating. Bill conformed with peers who drank excessively, though once therapy began, he compartmentalized, binging on weekends and rigidly refraining from drinking weekdays in order to study. He and the therapist continue to work on this problem and attempted to examine his steadfast refusal to attend campus Alcoholics Anonymous (AA) meetings. Slavish peer conformity caused him not only to drink, but to conceal his passionate interest in classical music. He would semisecretly seek out music rooms on campus and would practice and play the piano for hours. Bill related his discomfort when classical music was scorned by peers. "When they knock Bach and Beethoven I felt like they attacked my close friends."

Clearly, Bill is struggling with identity formation and the necessary, age-appropriate separation and emancipation from his parents. He lacks a solid sense of self and the firm self-esteem to openly stand by his own values and preferences or to risk entering the coed world of his campus. Rather, he remains with male friends, eager to be part of the group. He rooms with a childhood friend from high school; obviously he could not overcome his separation fears in order to confidently enter into a living arrangement with strangers. Despite existent problems and delayed development, he was able to utilize the therapeutic relationship to calm down and master the academic challenges of the first freshman semester. Continued therapy should deepen and further better coping and adaptation.

Bill's situation is far from unique. The positives are apparent, in that he was able to share his anxieties with his parents and enlist their aid in finding him help. Many college students do not share concerns with parents, but rather turn to peers, dorm resident supervisors, advisers, professors, peer counseling services, and campus mental health services. Some students unfortunately ignore and deny their problems with disastrous results. Promptly seeking help serves as an excellent preventative or an early intervention and staves off more regression and anxiety. When help is not sought, problems generally increase to overwhelming proportions: papers cannot be completed, and tests cannot be faced or passed. The root of the academic difficulty is not a matter of intelligence, but rather handling independent living and managing sexual feelings, frustration, anxiety, and depression. College is bound to produce disappointments and anxiety-inducing, challenging situations that overwhelm a small proportion of students. This group often has perfectionistic standards due to poor self-esteem. So much is expected that nothing is good enough except straight A's and a stupendous career. Little is attempted out of fear of trying and failing. Some students handle the academic work, but manifest serious problems and symptoms in non-school-related ways. These may involve substance abuse, eating and sleeping disorders, depression, and social withdrawal. Such symptoms may be due to poor self-esteem, separation problems, or sexual concerns.

Sexual feelings and sexual behaviors pose major problems for older adolescents. The value system of our rapidly changing culture is constantly challenged and changing in response to the changing views, behaviors, and realities of today's youth. Adolescents of all ages, especially older adolescents, have been affected by the sexual revolution and the current cult of immediacy that emphasizes instant gratification. For some there is little distinction between sexual and aggressive expression. Some young people at college, living away from home for the first time, frenetically seek someone to feel close to and depend on out of fear of being alone. Some fall in love and feel overwhelmed by erotic arousal and physical intimacy. Some are offhanded and self-absorbed in seeking sexual satisfaction; they may share their rooms with sexual partners and be oblivious to the needs and wishes of same-sex roommates. Some relationships are monogamous; some young adults engage in nonexclusive dating patterns. The sexual freedoms that accompanied the widespread use of the pill and other "safe" contraceptives altered previously established rules, but this new freedom is now in question, following the recognition of the epidemic proportions of sexually transmitted diseases. Fear of disease, especially AIDS, has

prompted many older youth to abandon their uncommitted, freewheeling approaches to sex. Despite recent
cautions, however, experimentation goes on, and college
students worry about their sexual attractiveness and adequacy. A crucial factor in the management of sexual
strivings is the older adolescents' sense of ownership of
the body. The issue seems to be whether the older adolescent can "affectively experience his mature body as
belonging to himself or whether he reacts to it as if it still
belonged to his mother who first cared for it" (Laufer
1968, p. 115). If they regard the body as the enemy, as
something quite separate from the rest of themselves, or
as nonexistent or free of danger, they may resort to such
things as substance abuse, eating disorders, and self-
mutilating acts.

Whatever the manifest problems and causes of adjustment difficulties the parent can and should remain connected and supportive, and not become excessively
discouraged. Difficult beginnings do not connote failure.
Hopefully, the adult child is not entirely successful in externalizing his sense of helplessness, which would cause
the parent to feel as overwhelmed as is the child. Steadfast,
committed, long-distance parenting is necessary during
the college years. Because parents can often do little directly, they need to support the help-seeking efforts of
their older adolescents. In extreme circumstances, they
must be compassionate in the face of their child's defeat
and his or her return home for an interval before being
ready to return to school. Despite parental anger and frustration, disappointed parents have to temper their own
despair and not become preoccupied with these issues.

Children having successfully "dumped" their emotional baggage, must not get off unscathed nor feel unperturbed by the mess that has often been created. Parents err if they attempt to cover up or to shield their children from the consequences of their behavior, for example, by trying to circumvent the rulings of the school in cases of expulsion for substance abuse, plagiarism, and the like. The same problematic situation will recur in instances where the parent bail out child. Genuine learning of consequences, and right and wrong is further delayed by overprotective, overly indulgent parents. Some young people have to learn the hard way; after years of turning a deaf ear to parental advice and admonishment, they need to face the logical results of their actions and inactions.

In addition to the academic, sexual, and social demands of college life, there are challenges of time and money management, which involve allowances, personal earnings, part-time employment, and summer employment. Economic resources and personal attitudes toward money affect how this is handled by each family. Again the key for parents is "not too much and not too little." Unlimited use of credit cards and an endless supply of money do little to help college students handle their affairs in a mature and responsible fashion. Excessive monies, and excessive belongings like cars, clothes, cameras, computers, and sports equipment, may produce the irresponsible attitude of "there's more from where that came." Those with the most generally take the worst care of belongings. Monetary indulgences can cripple initiative and the sense of being self-supporting and self-sufficient. Many college students from less affluent homes, work part time while in college to cover their expenses; the job serves to provide them needed funds and enhanced self-esteem. Some students simply cannot balance a job and an academic program; they cannot optimally handle their school work while employed. The needs and varied capacities of students are enormous, for work and study must also be balanced with campus life, including involvement in sports and student activities, like theater and student newspaper. The best experience is one in which students are neither overindulged nor massively frustrated, for example, by being deprived of all school-based activities because of financial need for extensive employment while in college. A number of colleges have combined work–study programs, which can often be the best solution for those who need to work during college.

The college years have the potential to facilitate great personal and intellectual growth. Experimentation and inquiry abound; students are challenged by new ideas, exciting fields of study, and social and philosophical exchanges with peers and professors. "The reliance once vested in the parent now becomes attached to the self, and sacrifices of all kinds are made in order to sustain a sense of dignity and self-esteem" (Blos 1962, p. 152). Ideally during post-adolescence, individuals find a niche in some section of their society that is firmly defined yet seems uniquely made for them. This provides young adults an ensured sense of inner continuity and social sameness that bridges what they were as children with what they are about to become and reconciles their conception of themselves with their family's and community's recognition (Erikson 1950, 1956). The college years impose significant demands, and under favorable circumstances, there is a consolidation of the sense of self, as well as a choice of long-term goals and guiding ideals in harmony with the goal-directed aspirations of the self (Kohut 1978).

Late adolescence is a decisive turning point and consequently has been viewed by many researchers as a time of crisis. The outcome depends on young persons' ego capacities, conscience, moral values, and the demands of the external world. For some, this can be a time of high psychic mortality because of individual vulnerabilities and the pressures and inordinate cultural demands for good grades, admission to graduate school, or a good entry-level job. Some young people feel more confident, better educated, and better prepared for life after college. Amid all the struggles for selfhood the birth of the adult slips in quietly, with none of the drama and violence of the original birth and no burst of changes as at puberty and early adolescence. College-age students, for better or worse, have left the world of innocence and protection. The experiences and sense of self at the "portal of adulthood" continue with them and reverberate throughout the life cycle (Rangell 1990).

PART THREE

CHALLENGES TO PARENTHOOD

9

Homework and School Achievement: Whose Homework Is It Anyhow?

As in many other aspects of parenting, there is a range of opinions and advice about the appropriate parental responsibility and response toward children's homework. Dr. Ron Taffel (1991) urges parents not to send children to an isolated, quiet place to do their homework. His rationale is that many children object to isolation and separation and prefer to work near noise and in everyone's earshot. Additionally, he recommends that parents monitor and engage with children in executing homework, unless it causes terrible struggles or means more to parents than to children so that parents end up doing the work. By contrast, Dr. Haim Ginott (1956) recommends that parents not supervise or check homework except at the child's invitation. He cautions that this realm of a child's life is a child's responsibility, not the parents', and that the sole value of homework is to give youngsters the experience of working on their own. The expectation of autonomous academic functioning begins in some schools in the early grades. Like many educators, Dr. Ginott believes parents should not actively engage in the process, beyond providing indirect help in selection of a regular time and place for study.

In some households, parents and children engage in nightly battles over homework; in others, the arguments center on children's insistence on, and parents' objectives to, homework accompanied by television, stereo, and telephone. Many parents gnash their teeth over their children's hastily done, sloppy, or repeatedly "forgotten" homework. Dawdling, rushing, or last-minute demands for help on a big project not completed the night before it is due are common phenomena at all grade levels. Parents try various strategies and often feel exhausted and defeated because nothing seems to work. There are no simple, quick answers; the process of negotiating and supporting this area of your children's life is a lengthy one.

While some parents do not take lower-grade homework seriously and dismiss it as "busy work," most parents and educators regard homework as important and significant for children's current and future academic performance. Research demonstrates that consistent attention to homework produces much better students than those who ignore this expectation for independent study. For most children, homework is the first thing they are responsible for on their own. This responsibility of childhood is greatly influenced by parents' motivation and support. Successful students seem to have parents whose attitudes show they care about their children's schoolwork. Such parents convey that their children's education is a family priority and that homework is a major part of that priority (Canter and Hausner 1987).

Parents are commonly cautioned by most writers not to teach concepts or routinely correct their children's work, but they are encouraged to establish a disciplined, supportive learning environment in the home.

A developmental and individualized perspective seems to offer more answers for parents than global injunctions that often are very difficult to put into effect. As small children need more proximity to parents, what is appropriate and what works for them differ greatly from what is age-appropriate for a pubescent or older adolescent. The space and circumstances of family life are also so varied that no rule can actually be applied across the board. Some youngsters have their own room, and others share a bedroom with a sibling. Some live in compressed quarters, and others have a wide range of choices about where to work, for instance, a den, a library, their bedroom, a kitchen table, or a breakfast room. Whatever the choice, a special pace used routinely seems generally preferable to children's wandering about to find a spot. The actual location is less significant than whether or not there is freedom from distraction.

Young, primary-grade children rarely want to go off alone to their room; they prefer to be near their parents. If they need help or have questions, they want to ask the parent, just as they do the teacher in the classroom. Some children keep their crayons, scissors, and pencils in their room, whereas others leave their "tool box" in the breakfast room, wherever they work. Getting situated in a routine site helps to organize children so that they are not dashing off to find a pencil, markers, and the like, in the jack-in-the-box pattern that disrupts concentration and the flow of ideas. Lower-grade children rarely are expected to do long assignments. A single sitting, or two at most, should suffice for them to complete their work thoroughly and appropriately.

Trying to work in the center of chaos is hardly realistic for a person of any age. Working at the kitchen table while the mother prepares supper may be possible in an only-child home, but would be unsuitable when the mother attends to several siblings in the kitchen as well as preparing dinner. Children doing homework are *not* the center of the universe. All else need not stop when work is in progress. When children practice the piano, for example, family members do not go mutely tiptoeing about, nor can they do so when homework is being attended to by one member. Working children should be in a site apart from their mother's phone conversations, a sibling's television cartoons, or other siblings' play space. Parents must help them find a routinely used, comfortable, well-lit place where there is little distraction. Young children cannot decide when to do their homework; inflexible rules rarely work because the season of the year and extracurricular activities commonly alter the best-laid schedules. Young children need to relax and play following school and rarely can attend to homework as soon as they get home. Given their working schedules, parents cannot realistically expect young children, or the in-house caregiver, to assume total responsibility for the execution of homework. What is important is that homework not be left as the last item on the daily agenda, to be done late in the evening when youngsters are fatigued and unable to concentrate. While they working, younger and older children should understand the television, play, and phone calls must be deferred. Organized parents arrange daily homework time for the younger child, in the same way that a schedule is made for biweekly hockey and a weekly music lesson. Thus a primary-grade youngster may be expected to do homework from 5:30 P.M. to 6:30 P.M. routinely, except on soccer or ice-hockey days when study time is 7:00 P.M. to 8:00 P.M. Homework must not be viewed as punishment or banishment, but as part of daily living, to be completed with as much independence as possible.

Rigid supervision or daily correction of work executed sets up dependency patterns, as does hurried handling of children's questions, when parents always give the proper answer to word definitions or spellings. Even at a young age, children should be expected and encouraged to use a dictionary as they do in the classroom. Teachers are not at school to offer instant answers, bur rather to assist children in finding the answer themselves by directing them to maps, dictionaries, and research texts. Ideally, more patient and thoughtful parents do the same. The fastest course is not the best course; parents must take time to encourage children to persevere in the search for information as independently as possible. Encouragement and praise from parents are important; they stimulate youngsters to seek and expect the same from the teachers at school. Praise cannot be false, and parents need to be realistic about standards and not compliment a child for a messy, careless handling of the assignment. On the other hand, angry and critical responses obviously do not work. Restraint and firmness are important when parents offer assessment or instruction on how to produce a neater paper.

Many young children want parental help or checking when they prepare for a spelling quiz or a test on multiplication tables. If it is apparent that errors abound and that the child has not memorized what is expected, parents wisely disengage and encourage the child to work independently to master their assignment before involving the parents in review. Many children rush through assignments carelessly, in a hurry to make phone calls or to watch a television program, and claim they are done in half the prescribed homework interval. They must be held to the task for the full allotment of time and be shown that *no one* can master the assignment *properly* in just a few minutes.

Because homework is children's introduction to independent responsibility, it must be executed by them on their own. They must master the necessary skills, learn to follow directions, and begin to thoroughly complete a task. Management of homework helps them to learn to manage time and to anticipate what is entailed in long-range assignments that require planning to get to a library, find the appropriate reference books, do the needed research before writing the report or paper. When parents overhelp, they hurt children and deprive them of a critical aspect of learning. Grades are less important than independently mastering what in fact is their age-appropriate job. Children often complain that the work is too hard or that the teacher did not explain the assignment. Sometimes this account is accurate, but in other instances, children may need encouragement because their apprehension makes everything initially feel too hard. Whatever the reason for a slow or hesitant approach, parents err greatly when they complete the task for children. From early on, children must learn to persevere. They must be encouraged not to expect instant success and mastery. It is often necessary and helpful to point out to them that they persevere and practice in other areas of their life with eventual success and mastery, in shooting baskets, in perfecting a dive at the swimming pool, and so on.

The independent handling of schoolwork does not preclude answering questions and, if needed, reviewing directions to help get children engaged in the work process. Often parents can help young children order their approach to assignments by encouraging them to start with their hardest or least favorite topic. It is not wise to offer problem-solving help until children have tried to solve the question on their own. Homework helps develop frustration tolerance and perseverance; when parents too readily jump in with assistance, they stifle initiative and may produce negative, even disastrous, results. Some children never develop confidence in their capacity to work alone.

Children may stop and start their homework, become distracted with phone calls, and drag out the process until past an appropriate bedtime. When such activity becomes a pattern, parents are forced to intervene actively, for instance, by insisting that bedtime be adhered to and that children go to school unprepared unless they choose to arise early. Other interventions require supervision and curtailment of telephone use or incentives like a ping-pong game with a parent when work is done. Sometimes nothing works short of getting tough and firm. Holding the line and insisting that children work on their own for better or for worse are at times the only recourses if children use anger, tears, blackmail, or resistance to try to manipulate parents into doing their work for them. Parents cannot *make* children do their work, but they can confront them with consequences and choices. They can lose all television and phone privileges and sit all evening over their work if they choose and if the work is not completed, they can go to school unprepared and face the consequences in class and at home after parents confer with the teacher by phone or in person. Parents must back up their words with actions, be consistent, and follow through. It is important not to make meaningless threats of punishments or to discuss or attempt to execute punitive measures, like spankings or isolation. Children test parents, for instance, by using the phone. Their calls must be interrupted and curtailed, and your warning must be carried out, despite anger and rebellion on your children's part.

Sometimes young and older children have to be faced with harder choices and consequences, like losing privileges for extracurricular activities if their "job" is ignored. Parents must convey the reality that work comes before play and that if homework is ignored, secondary things like Little League or the hockey team will have to go until the children assume age-appropriate responsibility. Children's choice, not an angry threat that is not carried out, must be presented. Consequences should be prompt and immediate; determined in a nonimpulsive, nonangry fashion, carefully thought out with advance planning and parental collaboration. It is useless and counterproductive to ground children for a month or two or to threaten such a punishment. Rather, a rational, calmly articulated set of choices is appropriate.

Some children need professional help, like tutoring or therapy, in situations where resistance and poor performance persists. Sometimes a child's resistance is based on an undetected learning disability, which may interfere with the handling of specific courses or work. Assessment by a trained child specialist is the most effective way to evaluate a child's work inhibitions and academic underachievement. Generally the best beginning point of consultation is with the school and the children's teacher. Good teachers are receptive to calls and contacts with parents; they greatly appreciate the parents' interest, the information parents can provide, and the parents' desire for the teacher's observation and input. Knowing that home and school have allied helps children succeed. When parents remain unresponsive to low marks and deficiency reports, teachers can only conclude that parents are indifferent to their children's school performance. Teachers need to be informed if there are problems at home or dramatic changes (such as divorce, an anticipated family move, illness of a parent) that might explain a child's decline in his or her academic and social adjustment. In more routine situations, it is important to contact the teacher when children cannot do or complete homework assignments, neglect to bring home assigned

work, exhibit very poor work habits, are bored, unhappy, or socially estranged, or are continually frantic
and anxious about school and homework.

By middle school and high school, children are expected to work in an increasingly independent fashion.
At this point, demands are greater, and increased solitude
in their room is important for concentration. Indeed
children are generally taking courses that parents are
unfamiliar with and unable to assist them with. Many
parents know little about computers, various higher
math and science courses, or the foreign language their
children have chosen to study. The assignments are increasingly complex and demanding and may be long-
term research projects. Some high schools have rigorous
finals and final week, all to prepare children for the
actuality of college. Organizational skills, good study
habits, and the ability to manage time are, it is hoped, in
place. Nevertheless, some adolescents show an academic
decline after a history of solid and continuous performance, and this often requires that parents again exert
limits to allow responsible management of homework
and express expectations about school performance.

Some high-school and middle-school children cut
classes, ignore homework assignments, or claim they
have finished their work in study hall. Older children can
often cover their tracks, but on the day of reckoning,
deficiency reports or marginal or failing grades on report
cards arrive in the mail. Some adolescents go to all
lengths to conceal their poor performance, getting to the
mailbox before parents to retrieve the deficiency report,
and concealing messages and calls from teachers to par-

ents. Alert parents should be aware of trouble and not need actual notice from the teacher. If they see no work being done at home, they should wonder and not be lulled or misled by children's account of work completed in study hall. If their teenagers live on the phone and go out on school nights, age-appropriate work is clearly not being attended to. Parents do not want to become intrusive, but they should not ignore what in fact is happening.

Limits, consequences, and choices are now of a different order. Parents cannot force adolescents to do their work, to study, or to attend classes faithfully and punctually. Threats and angry exchanges are understandable but of little avail. What is important is communication in the form of efforts to discuss school with children and to better understand what is happening and why. Some adolescents are unusually susceptible to peer pressure and will conform to the group mores, which may involve "blowing off" school. When depressed and unhappy, some adolescents feel they no longer can compete; they may change friendships and mix only with other youth who have disengaged from learning and academic achievement. Sometimes marked academic decline and change of friends signify more than adolescent moodiness and generalized discontent. Youngsters may be engaging in some experimentation with substance abuse or may be seriously involved in drinking and drug use. Parents need to inform themselves about what is going on and not avoid conflict by sidestepping the issues apparent in poor grades and questionable friendships. Their expression of concern shows a desire to help and often stimulates a renewed and improved dialogue. Depending on what is learned, parents can often determine whether the situation will self-correct or require professional consultation. Some adolescents who are doing poorly in school are reacting to particular home-based problems, such as marital conflict or their father's being laid off from his job. Whatever the reason, parents' compassionate but firm evidence of concern and interest is crucial for improving the situation. Falling behind is serious, and parents need to attend to children's distress even if confronted with their own life stressors. Parents attending to children despite divorce proceedings, for example, demonstrates that they are doing their job. Such behavior is a good model for children and demonstrates that they too must do their job, their school work, despite unhappiness about family problems. It is important that problems and unhappiness not become bases of entitlement to avoid responsibility!

Aside from personal or family-centered stress or unhappiness, some adolescents suffer academic decline for other reasons. Extracurricular interests may take precedence; the immediate gratification on the football field and basketball court, at the school theater, or with a rock band can completely overshadow any sense of responsibility about academics and homework. It would be ill-advised for the parent to impulsively prohibit involvement in these wholesome pursuits: such an act may humiliate and enrage the child, and there's little chance that the freed-up time would be productively rechanneled into homework and study. The wisest course entails respectful discussion between parents and adolescents, to consider better ways to manage time and to become more responsible about schoolwork while engaging in the extracurricular passion. Some reassessment of priorities is necessary, and alterations are clearly in order. There are possible solutions and compromises. Discussion between parents and children may result in an agreement that after the basketball or football season, adolescents will refrain from trying out for the next season's sport and will re-immerse themselves in appropriate, responsible study. Theater-struck students will agree not to try out for the next production and will waive involvement in production and stage crew until the summer internship at the local theater. Rock musicians will opt for a lighter academic load next semester, augmented by attendance at summer school. Year-long earnings are generated by the rock band's fees, and the parent shows respect for both the income-generating work and the son or daughter's musical enthusiasm. In all of these instances, the parent–child exchange demonstrates mutual respect and articulation of the different and distinct values of each party. The parent does not dismiss the adolescent's athletic, musical, or theater interests as unimportant, but also does not waiver about the importance of academics. Adolescents are helped to compromise, make choices, defer endless instant gratification, and reconnect with the primacy of their age-appropriate, responsible handling of their job, namely, school obligations. Such problem solving prepares adolescents for similar choices they will face at college, with the array of activities and programs in addition to their course of study.

Some adolescents are more comfortable in specialized school settings where their interests are incorporated into the curriculum. Many public and private programs specialize in music and art, the performing arts, fashion and design, science, math, computers, and so on. Some innovative programs in urban public-school systems have "schools without walls" programs, whereby schoolwork and planned internships are integrated and are coordinated by the school in tandem with local theaters, newspapers, museums, banks, medical research laboratories, hospitals, social services agencies, computer centers, publishing houses, or television stations. Some adolescents thrive in this combination of study and immersion in their area of interest.

Whatever the school or schedule, the goal of school and homework is that of independent management of study, social life, and extracurricular interests. Homework is more than sitting over an assignment. It is about learning to make choices; about how, where, and when to do homework, how to study, what to study, and with whom to study. While homework is basically solitary, it often involves group and team projects and research endeavors, beginning in middle school and continuing through college. Thus, homework involves cognitive skills, intelligence, social skills, listening, and sharing ideas. Students must often collectively synthesize concepts, trends, and varied interpretations of literature, social phenomena, research-project findings, or symbolism in poems or paintings.

The out-of-class study in college is not the same as homework of younger years. Rather, it is independent study, preparation, research, or creative endeavor. Parents have minimal influence on college students' management of school responsibilities. Their efforts of the earlier years were to provide support, encouragement, and supervision, all to prepare children for independent, responsible management of life and learning away from home. Some youths, who have been oversupervised earlier, let loose and demonstrate an unevenness or inability in handling their work responsibility when they enter college. Often this initial floundering is temporary and quickly corrected. In other situations, the wrong choice of subjects causes disinterest and confusion; grades plummet until a more congenial course of study is selected. Some students find it hard to avoid the distraction and socializing in dorms; they overindulge in late-night activities with friends and put off attending to their work or even attending classes. Often they regress to earlier maladaptive patterns such as avoidance of difficult work, procrastination, last-minute, sloppy preparation, and panicky "all-nighters" before exams. Undisciplined youths boast or complain that they can work only under the gun. For a multitude of reasons they avoid a more organized, thorough approach to study.

The consequences, of course, are theirs, and the significance of their grade point average has real ramifications for graduate school admission and for entering the job market. Even at a college level, those who graduate with honors and on time have enhanced resumes. Long-distance calls between college students and parents should not be an inquisition about grades and achievement, but clearly the engaged parent registers interest

and support. In the event that things do not go well,
parents must intervene. An aggressive tirade will only
turn off older adolescents, who become defensive and
angry. This sequence cancels what should be the students' appropriate guilt and concern. If the parent erupts
and takes over the worry and concern, then their older
adolescent is improperly unburdened and relieved from
what in fact *is* his or her burden and responsibility. The
calm, firm parent stimulates the adolescent's conscience by
registering clear concerns, not by angry sermons to initiate guilt.

Sometimes efforts at empathic inquiry and calm discussion fail, and students close off from discussion.
Parents cannot badger but can firmly state that a reassessment in planning is on the agenda next visit home. It is
best to conserve breath and energy and only discuss
matters when parents are listened to. Parents need not
feel helpless and impatient about the situation; in fact,
they are not powerless. They are paying the bills and are
entitled to have opinions and preferences on how their
money is spent. When parents sacrifice and scrimp to
underwrite their child's college education, it is only natural for them to feel exploited and angry that these
monies are being squandered. It is counterproductive to
explode and threaten to curtail paying the bills, but it is
realistic and reasonable to firmly and calmly articulate
feelings, specific values, and standards about academic
achievements and adolescents' lifestyle in college. Parents are within their rights to offer clear and unequivocal
choices, when their son or daughter is clearly not working. Poor academic performance demonstrates adoles-

cents' lack of responsibility or readiness for college, and taking off a semester or a year to work may be an alternative. Other alternatives are local junior colleges or less expensive local schools where adolescents earn part of their school expenses. Parents have a right to expect their adolescents' best efforts in college; adolescents may choose different priorities, but only at their own expense. Even at the college level, some students learn only the hard way and are able to turn things around only when confronted with parental limits. Others simply are not ready for autonomous independent living and need more time for maturation. Some college students have serious social and academic difficulties due to emotional problems, and these situations require professional outside help.

Any genuine school achievement is predicated on what Winnicott (1958) called "The Capacity To Be Alone." This capacity is one of the most important signs of maturity in emotional development. It is paradoxically linked with relatedness. The capacity to be alone is the experience of being alone while someone else is nearby. Despite being alone, the presence of the other is important. This phenomenon occurs early in toddlerhood when the child plays independently, comforted by the knowledge of the mother's presence nearby. Later in life, older children and young adults can work and enjoy solitude and privacy without feeling any loss of relationship with parents, intimate friends, professors or mentors, or romantic partners. This internal secure connectedness supports and affirms solitary activity and enables successful students to soothe themselves and work independently with perseverance and confidence.

10

Working Mothers:
Myths and Reality

Today's economic and social realities require many
women to work because their income is needed for the
family or because they are single mothers with major
financial pressures. The percentage of mothers who are
employed full time is ever increasing; the majority return
to work when children are under a year old. In 1970, in
40 percent of families, both husband and wife worked.
By 1990 the percentage had increased to 60 percent.
Changes in American family life were central to the 1992
presidential campaign, exemplified by some politicians'
attacks on single motherhood and Bill Clinton's promises of increased economic support for working families.

Few people are wildly ecstatic about the version of the
Family and Medical Leave Act that will go into effect. . . .
Many businesses would like no version of the measure,
which requires them to grant employees up to twelve
weeks of unpaid leave a year for family medical emergencies, arguing they already shoulder more than their share
of expensive Washington-imposed social policy. Em-
ployee advocates wanted a stronger version, along the
European model of extended paid leave, pointing out

that few workers can afford to forego a paycheck for
three months. . . . The Family and Medical Leave Act of
1993 requires employers with fifty or more employees to
grant up to twelve weeks of unpaid leave annually, according to the Labor Department, for the birth or adop-
tion of a child, to care for a spouse or an immediate family
member with a serious health condition or inability to
work because of a serious health condition. [Noble 1993]

The middle class confronts new domestic and economic uncertainty, but perhaps more unsettling is the
painful, recent recognition of unmet expectations. The
current erosion of the American dream is viewed by
many as caused by escalating housing costs, occupational
insecurity, few career ladders because of few opportunities for job advancement, and the increasing pressures
created by the rising cost of living. These realities are
hard to manage, even by well-educated, well-trained
adults. The need for added family income affects families
across the socioeconomic continuum, and thus the majority of mothers are employed, be they lower class,
working class, middle class, or upper middle class and
professionally trained.

Professional women who have invested inordinate
years in graduate school and training can rarely take a
full-time hiatus from their profession. They often feel
torn by their children's and their own professional aspirations and gratifications, even when not propelled by
economic pressures. It is the rare professional woman
who can arrange a part-time work schedule to spend
significant time at home with an infant or toddler. Studies
have demonstrated that work–family conflict is not a

gender issue, but rather is related to family roles and responsibilities allocated traditionally, according to gender. Changes are underway in dividing roles and responsibilities. Nevertheless, the work–family conflict generally occurs for a man when he loses his job and for a woman when she takes a job.

Some contemporary writers, like their earlier counterparts, advocate staying home for the first year; others recommend that in the best interest of children, mothers should stay at home for the first 3 years (White 1979, 1984). The basis of these authors' conclusions is that parents provide children with a better start in life. They do not believe any substitute care or caregiver can "match the enthusiasm and excitement of parents over a baby's accomplishments . . ." (Baldwin 1989, p. 127). Because the unique parent–child bond is formed in the first 2 years of life, the baby who is cared for by parents or family members develops a deep sense of self-worth and security. David Elkind (1984) cautions about the high level of anxiety that results when children are pushed to cope with things beyond their years, for example, excessively early separation and group child care with an inadequate ratio of adults to children.

Despite these perceptions of optimal child development, reality generally commands full-time maternal employments; part-time arrangements and work at home are rarely possible. Many other writers recommend that the best alternative is individual care in the child's or another person's home. The next best is family day care, then nonprofit, center-based care. The last alternative is profit-oriented, center-based care that is a

franchise whose teachers are unfortunately generally un-
dertrained and poorly paid. Fathers or grandparents are
considered the best alternative to maternal care. However, it is the rare household where a father can serve as a
house husband or can work at home. Even when this
alternative is possible, additional child-care help is commonly required to enable the father to work at home, be
it at music making, painting, writing, computer consultation, or whatever the home-based work activity. In
sum, there are many variations of child care for employed
mothers to seek out and evaluate.

Handling the demands of full-time work and part-
time parenting calls for optimal creativity, efficiency, and
organization; ideally, both parents provide child care and
divide and conquer the tasks of homemaking. Cooking,
shopping, bill paying, cleaning, and child care are each
considerable tasks. The single mother is commonly the
most burdened of all in today's society. The support of
friends and grandparents is invaluable for all parents,
especially the single parent, who in some circumstances
may be the father rather than the mother. Parenting and
full-time employment become more demanding when a
family is composed of several children or part-time children, in cases of divorce with visitations, commonly on
weekends. Recently, there has been an increase in joint
custody, whereby children split the week and live half
time with each parent. Whatever the family composition,
it is crucial to provide as consistent and nurturant an
environment as possible; the expectations and burdens
fall more commonly on the working mother than on her
spouse (Apter 1993).

Some working mothers rely on extracurricular activities to compensate for their extensive absence. Such programs can provide enrichment if they are not offered too early. Elkind (1984) cautions against "mis-education" by too early enrollment in academic, music, and ballet classes. Children, especially young ones, need time at home to do nothing or to be relaxed and free to engage in imaginative play. Too much pressure to achieve in academics, sports, or the arts can generate insecurity and anxiety. Children similarly do not benefit from overstimulation by excessive movie or television watching. Television can be the bane of many households, especially when parents overrely on it for babysitting or distracting children, at times that parents feel harried by housework and simultaneous demands from several children.

Winn, in her book *The Plug-in Drug* (1985), states that heavy television viewing develops the right hemisphere of the brain at the expense of the left. The left hemisphere controls verbal and rational thought; the ability to read and write; to reason, organize ideas, and conceptualize them with spoken words and in writing. Excessive television viewing bombards watchers with images that rarely require thinking and rarely allow time to think. Such television viewing leaves little time for reading, playing, and engaging in sports and creative activities. "Radically limiting your child's television watching before the age of ten or eleven is probably one of the most far-reaching gifts you can give him or her developmentally" (Baldwin 1989, p. 229). It is easier said than done, but many believe that television should not be easily accessible to small children. If and when alternatives are made to decrease TV time, parents will need to put more time into family activities because it will take a while for children to become self-motivating and to use freed-up time creatively.

It takes hard work to establish a rhythm and balance in family life that provides supports and structure for parents and children. Baldwin (1989) offers a piece of critical advice, that is applicable to all parents, namely the importance of parents' attention to their own life and emotions, since the emotional tone in the home is far more important than the material environment. Thus the marital relationship, adult friendships, and work satisfactions cannot be overlooked if working parents hope to use themselves effectively, in life's crucial tasks of work, love, and leisure. Parenting involves all three throughout the stages of child rearing.

Working mothers commonly have problems exerting consistent discipline, due to reported guilt over their full-time work schedule. Many acknowledge being lax and permissive as an attempt to compensate for the lengthy daily separation. Out of the desire for a loving connection, discipline is too often surrendered to enable parent and child to supposedly enjoy quality time, enrichment, stimulation, and enjoyable togetherness. Often this hoped-for enjoyable exchange does not occur, and children remain irritable and rebellious. Children, especially young ones, require limits as well as connectedness and empathic understanding. Many small children cannot put feelings into words and respond to their mother's return from work with varying degrees of oppositional behavior. They are unable to articulate anger about the absence. They act it out because they cannot talk it out. Generally, mothers are shaken by this response to their return home. Often the negative behavior abates when the mother articulates the hypothesis that "perhaps Jimmy is angry, since the day and the wait for Mom felt long."

Helping a child put feelings into words facilitates that child's mastery and maturation. The optimal approach at the end of the day is to encourage words over whining and resistive actions. Encouraging children to join their mother in dinner preparations, for example, provides an avenue for a shared activity and a certain amount of recognition for accomplishment. Children's activity and play are serious and it is essential to their growth to affirm their participation. This recognition extends to the smallest contribution, for instance, a 3-year-old who brings the paper napkins to the table. This engagement of children is often a good transition when a work-weary mother re-enters the role of homemaker. Training is difficult unless habits are established early and parents hold to expectations that hands are washed before meals, toys are picked up, and yelling during a parent's phone call or dinner preparation is taboo. Indulgence and inconsistency suggest that the task or the parental expectation is unimportant. Fighting is senseless and commonly backfires; parents must not drag children to the washroom, but rather encourage and accompany them. In the event that children resist, parents must calmly say that dinner together is delayed until all children's hands are washed, toys are picked up, and so on. Parents can relax

and talk together or start their meal, commenting that
they hope that the children soon will join them after the
tasks are completed. Nagging and fighting never produce the desired results, and haste generally makes waste,
for example, when parents clean up toys because they
can do it more quickly than children can. Overdoing
infantilizes youngsters and further exhausts the already
overburdened working mother. Overpermissiveness un-
intentionally deprives children of age-appropriate accomplishments that are the norm in day care or at nursery
school, where no adult will wait on children as do overpermissive parents on a daily basis.

Working mothers often have to surrender rigid or
overly fastidious emphasis on an immaculate home, perfectly ironed blouses, homemade baked goods, extensive
house renovations, and so on in order to handle the
demands of work and children. Children of working
parents need to have relaxed and available parents, who
are not immersed 90 percent of the time in work around
the home. Rather what is needed are parents who have
the leisure and inclination to talk to and play with them.
In households where there are several children, the complexity of their needs can be considerable. Sometimes
children's age-appropriate capacities and needs are unwittingly sacrificed by pressured working mothers. A
common mistake is burdening the oldest child with excessive responsibilities for young siblings. Other problematic situations develop when the less demanding
children get overlooked or are expected to sacrifice their
preferences to a more noisy and demanding sibling; an

exhausted mother feels it is easier "to give into Billy's tantrum" than to settle a sibling conflict more fairly and equitably. Such common family dynamics push one child to be overly conforming, nonassertive, and thereby frustrated, and simultaneously overgratify the more troublesome child and in essence reward and enable negative behaviors. The working mother may think she is conserving her energy and sidestepping avoidable conflict, but in fact she is unwittingly perpetuating what will become a greater problem of child care, sibling rivalry, and appropriate discipline.

Working mothers chronically feel rushed, overscheduled, and at times overwhelmed as they struggle to meet commitments on the job and at home. Children generally forgive anything in their mother except unreliability. Thus, promises must be kept, and punctuality is most important despite the parents' work pressures. Children of all ages feel frightened, and even forgotten about, if they are left waiting for the tardy mother to arrive from work and retrieve them from school, day care, or a play date at a friend's home. Many adults and older adolescents in therapy recount the sense of fear and helplessness of earlier childhood, when they were kept waiting for what felt like interminable intervals of time because their mothers were constantly late in retrieving them. These memories were also replete with the children's sound recognition of the anger and resentment teachers and others felt toward them and their mothers when they also had to stay late to cover leftover children. Parents, despite employment or professional obligations, must provide an element of permanence and security in the "racing fight of life" (Ross 1984). Ideally, fathers pitch in and share carpooling and delivery and pickup of children.

The element of security and reliability is especially important when youngsters are ill. Child care and work demands often conflict, but it is important for parents to empathize with the children's view of their world and with their common apprehensions when they are acutely ill. In such instances, a parent's taking sick leave is often the best course to alleviate a child's anxiety. This responsibility, like so many others, generally falls to the mother rather than the father. Children are resilient and can handle many challenges, stresses, and separations that are not excessive and beyond age-appropriate coping capacities, if they feel valued and affirmed by parents. They can vigorously and enthusiastically jostle for space in their parents' busy schedule, buoyed by pride and respect for the parents who demonstrate their attentiveness and empathy.

Sheer exhaustion generally plagues women more than men; in addition to the demands of their job, working mothers are commonly forced to assume the greater part of household and primary child-care responsibilities than are fathers. Juggling can create frayed tempers and anger. Scolding, yelling, and criticism can get out of hand, and no "advice" can modify the simultaneous reality demands of a car pool, laundry, squabbling children, and groceries to put away. Parental self-awareness is the only remedy to exhaustion and repeated temper eruptions. Parents generally can anticipate when they feel pushed to the edge. Some report warning signs, realizing that they feel on the verge of tears, that they are starting to shake or breathe faster, and that their words pour out like a torrent. Generally, parents, like children, need some time out; exiting until they feel in control is wise. Children can be sent to their room, or parents can remove themselves until they feel in control. In extreme cases, where parents fear severely spanking children, separation is essential until self-control is resumed. In a tumultuous family, a mother in parent guidance therapy was instructed to go to the phone, call her therapist, and leave a message, in order to regain composure and distance from the child before her controls broke down. The feeling of not being alone and overwhelmed comforted this vulnerable woman, who could rely on the reality that she would always receive a call back, as soon as possible, from her therapist. Some children will pursue parents or refuse to go to their room. This tactic requires tired and overwrought parents to insist on some interval of privacy to regain self-control and to enforce their privacy (if children are not too young to be left alone for 10 or so minutes) by securing the door of their bedroom or the bathroom if necessary. Parents need to self-soothe, to be able to think clearly, and to speak rationally and realistically. They must be determined to be in control and not vulnerable to being set off by an obstreperous child. Parents, not children, are the thermostat for regulation of temper and anger. This form of self-restraint sets an appropriate emotional tone in the household and offers a model of behavior that children are expected to respect and emulate.

At times the best efforts and intentions fail and parents

erupt. The only reasonable recourse is an apology by the parent, who must admit to having overreacted or to having displaced frustrations from work onto the child. Often a child's dreadful behavior is the real precipitant, and this needs to be pointed out, in tandem with the parents' open admission that their fury was, nevertheless, inappropriate and not helpful to themselves or the child. One can't make endless excuses or rationalize inappropriate eruptions, or in any way suggest entitlement to volatile or aggressive behavior; children will of course follow suit. "I slugged Sally because I had a hard day at school. I failed my spelling test, and all afternoon my teacher was after me for talking and not paying attention." Along with appropriate apologies, parents and children must absorb the reality that *no* outside stress entitles anyone to be abusive to another.

It is important not to succumb to "the understanding fallacy, whereby understanding the basis of a child's unhappiness is misconstrued as accepting unacceptable behavior" (Weisberger 1987). A parent may accurately recognize a child's lack of self-confidence as the basis of bullying a younger sibling, and it is not helpful to make this interpretation. Explanation of cause is less effective than pointing out the goals of behavior—for example, in this instance, to be the big boss, which must be discussed as an inappropriate goal since it was pursued with bullying and aggressive behavior. Being the older, more mature big brother must be demonstrated by self-control, age-appropriate behavior, and consideration of a younger sibling.

Because of the economic and employment realities of

the nineties, the majority of working mothers have to work full time. This is true across the socioeconomic spectrum, even for middle- and upper-middle-class households, and are dictated by the costs of today's health care, housing, taxes, and enormous future expenses like college and graduate school for today's young children. Additionally, husbands' jobs are less secure than a decade ago. Layoffs are common at every level in today's economy. Line workers and high-level executives are being let go as more and more companies and industries downsize. Becoming a partner in a law or accounting firm no longer brings the permanency of the recent past. Thus, women in the workforce have become less and less an anomaly. These realities may ease the guilt so many working mothers struggle with. As guilt fades, working women may surrender the "parent blame" dogma that has characterized child psychology for decades. To parent in today's world requires faith, compassion, and commitment.

Furthermore, parents must resolve the stress inherent in continuous negotiations with each other. Under the expectations for parenting performance and an increased workload, parents are deviating from societal stereotypes of men's and women's roles. Resolutions about the division of home-based labor and responsibility are a "very difficult and emotion-laden task for any couple and this is the task faced by dual-worker couples today" (Lein 1984, p. 62). Because of differences in pay scale, women generally receive less than male colleagues who do the same job. Under legal pressures, this pattern is very slowly changing. Yet despite the emergence of some equity in salaries, fathers' earnings tend to surpass those of mothers' in two-career homes, and this reality often creates an unfortunate devaluation of women's work or career compared to men's. The inevitable and unfortunate backlash is the assumption that because they receive a lesser salary than their partners, women should compensate by assuming greater responsibilities in the home. Many husbands deny this reflexive response, but it is the unspoken and enacted behavioral rule in the home and creates maternal exhaustion and overt and covert marital tensions.

There have been even more rapid changes in social attitudes on other issues. The stigma of therapy or securing professional consultation has waned. Participation in parenting workshops and support groups is on the increase. Optimally such groups begin with prenatal classes attended by both parents. These can be followed by parent-guidance workshops and seminars available at many schools and community and religious institutions. Such educational workshops and discussion groups acquaint parents with normal parent–child development and the inevitable and necessary changes in attachment inherent in child rearing. Special topics on nursing, toilet training, sibling rivalry, discipline, religious education, and homework are standard, as are special circumstances such as divorce or the death of a parent. These groups offer information and education before serious problems arise and may provide as well a congenial atmosphere where friendships and support networks develop. Parents generally gain insight and a better perspective about their own situation from listening to other parents: it is easier to be objective when evaluating and understanding other people's problems. Confidence can grow in such groups, which ideally provide understanding and mutual aid. Such support can nurture working mothers, the most overburdened of all parents today. Unfortunately, such parent-education groups are attended mainly by mothers because stereotypes continue to designate them as the primary caretakers, educators, and experts in child care.

Despite the gains of the women's movement, recent studies show that even with couples sharing a nontraditional orientation toward the division of labor on the basis of sex roles, the advent of parenthood calls forth a more traditional definition of their roles. Mothers, including working mothers, continue to view their own role much more as that of homemaker and primary caretaker for children and view their husbands' role principally as that of provider. Both parents presume that the father is not readily available to *equally share* parenting with his wife during the early parenting years, because of his particular concerns with his own career development. The American middle-class and upper-middle-class wife tends to expect her husband to treat her as an equal. She expects her husband to have a good deal of independence and initiative, and to be focused on his future success in his occupation; and in relation to her and the children she expects some measure of cooperation and sharing of responsibility. Reciprocally, the husband expects his wife to help in his plans for future economic and social success, notably by putting his success goals above any personal career or occupational goals of her own and by developing the social and domestic skills suitable to his particular occupational status. This lack of reciprocity about career often creates strains; it is the rare household where a wife's career is viewed on parity with her husband's.

In working-class families, career aspirations rarely preoccupy either parent. Rather, the emphasis is more on the here and now, day-to-day pressures: wives expect husbands to work steadily and do their best to bring in enough money to satisfy the family's needs. Although wives commonly also work, neither parent expects a radical change in basic economic or social status. Such families generally produce more children than their more affluent counterparts, and supports are expected from friends and relatives in time of need. Working-class mothers expect husbands' involvement with the extended and complicated networks of friends and relatives, but they expect less in the realm of child rearing. Working-class women generally do not expect to be treated as equals in the home; many decisions are relegated to fathers when mothers are preoccupied with the children's needs. Working-class husbands expect submission but also a good deal of nurturant care from their wives. Wives must be concerned with husbands' needs as well as those of the children; everything else is secondary. In these families, the accent is on festivity in family life, management of bills, and child rearing by the mother as sole caretaker.

A number of researchers examining role strain, overload, and depression in working women have suggested that the women's movement has created many unintended consequences. Because of new options open to women and the feminist critique of the "motherhood mandate" (Russo 1979), the movement has demoralized working-class mothers. These mothers do not have a wide range of opportunities and choices available and hence suffer lowered morale and decreased feelings of satisfaction and self-worth. The inherent strains of combining work, homemaking, mothering, and the duties of a wife and "kin keeper" are increased by their contemporary devaluation. When working-class wives' eventual pay and status exceed their husbands', serious and irreconcilable differences frequently arise. This is observed even in traditionally conservative working-class homes, where the women's movement has had relatively little impact.

The arrival of children calls forth traditional gender roles even for nontraditional couples, and mothers commonly perpetuate their conventional performance in the family drama as expressive, affiliative kin keepers. Professionally gratified mothers present new facets to their roles, but the transmission of stereotyped sex-role distinctions continues from one generation to the next (Chodorow 1978, Gilligan 1979).

A professionally trained working mother may have greater career opportunities with increased commitments, once children are in school all day. This can coincide with the leveling off of the husband's career, as he confronts the limits of his hopes and aspirations. Such differing experiences may affect not only the marital relationship, but also that of each parent with the children (Cohler and Boxer 1984). Many social psychologists and sociologists suggest that this disruption of the equilibrium is a basic cause of the high divorce rate today. As women move away from their prescribed roles and alter their value orientation, many feel relieved to be freed from earlier repression and from the masking of their aspirations. Some couples can weather the strain and anxiety generated by new role conflict and unfamiliar transactions; they compromise, negotiate a new level of complementarity, and thereby re-achieve equilibrium. The key appears to be the extent to which husbands and wives agree about women's career choices and active engagement in professional life. Other critical factors relate to consensus about issues of power, influence, and communication.

Some interesting and expected contrasts have been observed between working-class and professionally employed mothers' attitudes to parenting satisfaction. Less-educated women appear to enjoy caring for younger children more than for older children. The reverse is true among well-educated, employed mothers, who find greater enjoyment in parenting adolescents, presumably because less nurturance is needed, communication is more mature, and shared interests commonly exist. The generation gap appears wider between teens and their working-class, overburdened mothers. Professionally employed women generally have the economic base, household help, and leisure to engage in community and organizational activities once adolescents have departed for college. This source of satisfaction and engagement is not commonly available to working-class women, who experience greater stress at the time of the empty nest when children have departed from home for work and school. Often these women tend to look back with nostalgia to the earlier years of marriage and parenthood, the source of their lives' greatest satisfactions. The obvious distinction between gratification from a profession and resignation to the demands of a job accounts for the range of feelings about employment in the various segments of the contemporary female workforce.

11

Divorce: Changing Cultural Attitudes and Concerns

In the last fifty years, continuously changing cultural norms have altered the prevailing views about marriage and divorce. In the 1950s failure to assume and maintain the spouse role was taken to be a sign or symptom of parents' psychological problems. By the mid-1970s, marriage had come to be seen by many as only a potential mechanism for increasing happiness and psychological well-being. In the 1980s, society is seen as placing a decreasing importance on marriage, and correspondingly, there has been more acceptance of the increased divorce rate in the United States. This new acceptance results in less isolation of single individuals and single parents, and in changed perceptions of the family (Offer & Sabshin 1984b). Divorced individuals are no longer stigmatized as pathological for choosing not to marry or for giving up the married state. Acceptance of the phenomenon of divorce has increased, but a deeper recognition of its long-term effects on children has been stimulated by continuous research since the mid-1970s. Some of this research has been made available to the lay public through journalism articles and television interviews with specialists. These recent findings are less sanguine than the earlier thinking that divorce was better for children than was being raised in an unhappy home. In fact, divorced homes are neither more nor less stressful or beneficial than unhappy marriages. Each imposes its own stresses and strains.

Since the swell of divorces in the '70s and early '80s, no dramatic increase is evident; in the early '90s, a decline has even appeared. There has been increased recognition that many divorced families suffer from reduced stature with accompanying negative effects on economic, social, and psychological well-being of children. A high correlation of childhood depression and divorce has been noted. In addition to depression, divorce often produces more fragmented behavior and less imaginativeness and emotional and social maturity in children in the immediate years after the breakup. These aspects of loss are not necessarily permanent: many resilient children surmount the strains of family breakdown. Resilience appears to depend on three broad categories of variables: "(1) personality disposition in the child; (2) a supportive family milieu; (3) an external support system that encourages and reinforces a child's coping efforts and strengthens these by reinforcing the child's positive values" (Offer and Sabshin 1984b, p. 318). The sooner the family discord and divorce disputes can be resolved, the better it is for the child. Questions remain about how completely the adverse affects in early childhood may be reversed, but improved family relationships correspondingly improve the outlook for children's immediate and long-term psychological development.

Divorce can be viewed as a process that is divided into three phases: "(1) an initial phase of family stress; (2) a second phase dominated by the adversary legal process; and (3) a third phase of post-divorce restabilization" (Disenhuz 1979, p. 378). In the first phase of family stress when communication between parents breaks down, parental alliances collapse, and combative modes of interaction become apparent. Parents may try to fight privately, to protect children and to conceal conflicts. Once a separation is initiated and filing for divorce begins, there is a public acknowledgment of failure at reconciliation and resolution of family problems. The legal process dominates the second phase and can unfold with civility or intense acrimony. Issues of money (alimony, child support, and division of property), visitation, and custody of children are handled by adversarial procedures. Such a situation creates feelings of alienation, loneliness, uncertainty, and anger, while personal alliances and emotional supports change. The critical event is the judicial decision that culminates in a finalized divorce. The third phase is post-divorce restabilization with altered family roles, responsibilities, and changes in parents' goals, finances, and lifestyles. Ideally there is a new equilibrium, complete with stable financial arrangements, consistent parental visitation arrangements, and shared parenting responsibilities. This ideal is far from routine, and all too many divorces remain adversarial long after the legal termination of the marriage. Conflicts over power, money, and children can be unending, and the ghosts of the original family dynamics often continue, as parents play out the same themes and struggles.

Children are the most common focus of continued parental conflict. They can be misused as pawns, spies, or
clubs to batter the former spouse. Despite continued
acrimony, most "children of divorce continue to cling to
the fantasy of a magical reconciliation between his separating parents" (Wallerstein and Kelly 1980, p. 3). These
hopes for parental reconciliation can persist for many
years, "sometimes long beyond the re-marriage of one or
both parents" (ibid). This intense desire or fantasy persists in various disguises. While children have difficulty
surrendering their hopes, parents commonly struggle
with gradual and painful disequilibrium on the path to
better adjustment, eventually characterized by confidence in new roles and relationships. Concurrent with
the parents' efforts to stabilize their lives, children
struggle to form new relationships with each parent and
to sort out the polarization of feelings around the custodial and absent parents. Each parent can be idealized,
vilified, or both.

Young children generally respond to the dissolution of
the family with anger, neediness, and bewilderment, all
of which may be accompanied by an increase in regres-
sive behavior. Elementary-school-age children respond
with depression and immobilization; anger is generally
exhibited as a defense against their suffering and discomfort at being forced to return to a closer, more dependent
connection to the custodial parent, commonly the
mother. Adolescents attempt to distance themselves
from both parents and from the legal process, because of
loyalty conflicts.

Much can remain unsaid as the teenager attempts to

sort out feelings and fantasies, parallel to the parents'
hesitancy in discussing their own and their children's
feelings and reactions. Parents frequently find it very
difficult to explain the reasons for the decision to divorce,
and either shroud all in mystery, or overly concise statements like "Daddy and I have stopped loving each
other." Overly intellectualized explanations are often
offered. The age of the child makes the parents' dilemma
understandable, as does the wish not to defame the other
parent. The impermanence of love, in the aforementioned example, does little to explain anything to a bewildered child, who can easily come to fear the parents
similarly ceasing to love them. There is no formula to
appropriately explain divorce, since explanations are dependent on the child's age, level of comprehension, reality events in the pre-divorce home, and the parents'
relationships with the child. The explanatory process is
not a simple act that is quickly completed, but rather a
lengthy process over time. Many children, especially
during adolescence, feel stigma and shame about the
public failure of their family life, and may avoid discussion with the parents and with peers.

The mourning response to divorce is quite different
when compared to the response of children who have lost
a parent through death. Michael Rutter (1971) found
delinquency rates were nearly double for boys whose
parents had divorced as compared to those in intact
homes or homes in which a parent had died. "This suggests that it may be the discord and disharmony, rather
than the breakup of the family, as such, which led to
anti-social behavior" (Garber 1984, p. 184). Other re-

search has focused on the high rates of acting out, attention-seeking behaviors, and intensified seductiveness of adolescent girls from divorced homes, as compared to the behavior of daughters whose fathers had died. Death appears to produce depression and more inner-directed responses; in contrast, divorce stimulates more acting-out rebellion and antisocial behavior.

The extensive research and publications of Judith Wallerstein and Joan Kelly since the 1970s, culminating in their 1980 text *Surviving the Breakup: How Children and Parents Cope with Divorce,* reveal that while divorce can be highly beneficial for many adults, it is not better for children than an unhappy marriage except in instances of severe conflict, domestic violence, and abuse. The divorcing process proves to be considerably longer than these researchers had initially supposed. Generally, children do not view the divorced family as an improvement over the predivorce home. Few of the children studied agree with their parents' decision to separate. The majority reported that a "significant part of their childhood or their adolescence had been a sad and frightening time" (Wallerstein and Kelly 1980, p. 306). The children studied and followed by the researchers were a healthy population who were advancing normally in their age-appropriate tasks. They came from protective, white, middle-class homes, thus spared the economic and social stressors endured by so many children of divorce in the general population. Yet even then children reflected the lengthy staying power of the aftereffects of parental divorce.

Before the breakup, children often attempt to keep peace and reduce parental conflict. Many try to effect reconciliation before and after the divorce. Too often they have fantasies of responsibility for the marital conflict or the failure to reunite the parents. Some theorists suggest that children's antisocial behaviors are due to their effort to reunite their parents by unconsciously selecting misbehaviors that they semi-realize concern both parents. In this way they hope that shared alarm will bring them together in a renewed parental alliance. Patterns of hostility, isolation, rejection, and torn loyalties abound. Younger children, who have not consolidated a clear and firm sense of identity, are particularly vulnerable to these repeated, stressful patterns. In divorce as well as in the aftermath of a parent's death, children identify with the absent parent.

> The custodial parent realizes slowly and almost imperceptibly that the child has become the absent parent in miniature. Should the child continue to function well at home and at school, the custodial parent may be willing to overlook or even deny the changes. However, if the child has problems or shows unacceptable behavior and character traits, the custodial parent engages in a subtle and often not so subtle pointing out that the negative features stem from the child's development into just as bad, stupid, and irresponsible, dishonest, etc., a person as the non-custodial parent. Since identification is based on unconscious process, the child will become bewildered and confused by such accusations as he does not experience himself as being different than before. [Garber 1984, p. 190]

Children who experience parent loss generally have ambivalent feelings toward their parents (Garmezy

1986). When there is a remarriage, they have great loyalty conflicts and resist facing any replacement of the noncustodial or deceased parent. Such replacement requires relinquishing some part of their original tie to their absent father or mother. Considerable guilt may arise, along with loyalty conflicts and ambivalence that can reverberate on all future matters of choice. In older adolescents and young adults, the results of guilt commonly become apparent in regard to making vocational choices and marital decisions. In cases of divorce, custodial and noncustodial parents generally have different standards for behavior, discipline, and the like. Again, children are caught in struggles about loyalty and identification; they may prefer one parent, but feel guilty about their preference. "There are no safeguards and rituals of intact (or divorced) family life which soften the frustration and anger from the inevitable conflicts which permeate all parent/child relationships" (Garber 1984, p. 192).

The rejected partner in a divorce usually experiences frustration, anger, and depression. Because of shame, guilt, and lowered self-esteem, he or she commonly functions defensively and erratically, for instance, by making irregular child-support payments and disrupting visitation schedules. Some noncustodial parents withdraw completely or overindulge their children with excessive activities and presents. Research reveals that the majority of noncustodial parents, most commonly fathers, fear their children's disapproval and anger. This fear causes them to be excessively permissive in matters of discipline, defensive and angry about their actions, or regressed to such a degree that children are forced into an adult parenting role with them. All of these actions and inactions anger custodial parents, commonly mothers, who feel they must pick up the pieces after each visitation. A constant stressor on children of divorce is the conscious or unconscious parental request or demand that children align with them. This stressor produces despair, anger, depression, and a sense of helplessness in children of all ages, including the young adult child, a new population experiencing breakdown of their parents' marriages after 20 or 30 years. Many children appear to walk a thin line, trying simultaneously to please both parents. Inevitably, judgments occur and are accompanied by respect or disrespect, shame, and pity, for the separated parents. If loyalty demands are enormous, they can put children in a "state of total paralysis in daily functioning on one end of the spectrum, and to frantic acting-out on the other end. Either behavioral response seems better than to have to make a conscious guilt inducing choice demanded by one or both parents" (Garber 1984, p. 194). A high proportion of divorced parents seek some type of therapy, in recognition of their own and their children's needs. Parents whose spouse has died appear less self-doubting and more hurt, in contrast to divorced parents who generally feel misunderstood, betrayed, and often stigmatized.

TASKS OF PARENTING

The many studies by Wallerstein and Kelly and other divorce researchers point to the continuing psychological importance of *two* parents. While custodial parents' caretaking and psychological roles become more complex and increasingly central, absent parents' psychological role *does not* correspondingly decline. Even in cases of remarriage, when stepparents become prominent figures in children's lives, the significance of the biological parent does not greatly diminish. Despite the noncustodial parent's lessened influence in daily life, children who once lived with their two parents retain significant and complex ties to both. Even the totally unavailable absent parent persists in a child's life, in the form of a ghost or shadow on the family's life. The noncustodial parent can grow in importance post-divorce; some fathers describe and acknowledge more active and positive fathering after the separation than before, in the intact home. By contrast, when the noncustodial parent virtually abandons the child, that parent is rarely diminished in the child's view, and in fact, idealization and longing can persist. "Only a few children when they reached adolescence were able to counter-reject a rejecting parent with a conscious resolve to follow another road in their life by choosing to emulate another adult whom they had come to both love and respect" (Wallerstein and Kelly, 1980, p. 308).

The child's age, strengths, and resilience determine his or her parenting needs. Also of significance is the child's emotional health and level of functioning before the divorce. The nurturance provided in the earlier years will sustain a child for a while, but following the divorce, "good enough" parenting must continue to be available. Some overwhelmed parents, in the aftermath of the breakup, feel and are depressed and dejected, due to chronic emotional and economic overload. Thus they may need an array of supports and services from relatives, friends, and professionals to cope more effectively and to adequately meet their and their children's needs. Many children need, and profit from, individual and group counseling programs; others need day care and after-school care. Parents must be resourceful in finding the right supports and services for their children and themselves.

Wallerstein and Kelly (1980) differ from the position taken by Joseph Goldstein, Anna Freud, and Albert G. Solnit in their book *Beyond the Best Interests of the Child* (1973). Goldstein and colleagues recommended that the custodial mother have primary, if not total, control over making decisions regarding the child's needs, visitation, and so on. Wallerstein and Kelly (1980) stress both parents' central role in the psychological health of the child, whereby both parents need to be helped to provide input and continuity in child-rearing. Joint custody is viewed as far more than physical custody and apportioning of a child's residence and life. It is a concept and legal mechanism that provides two parents, in two separate homes, to care for children in a "post-divorce atmosphere of civilized, respectful exchange" (Wallerstein and Kelly 1980, p. 310). This arrangement can work in many cases, but in others, the inability to compromise or solve problems, the inability that led to divorce, continues afterward. With or without conflict, the continued availability and involvement of both parents is crucial for children's immediate and long-range well-being.

Parents often wonder if they should postpone divorce until children are older. Many recent dissolutions of long-lasting marriages are explained as the outcome of staying together until children are older and able to tolerate the end of the family and the parents' marriage. When parents decide to divorce, good outcomes are seen as uncorrelated to children's sex. Instead, the outcome depends primarily on "the child's relationship with each parent, the quality of life, within the divorced family and the extent to which the divorce itself provided the remedy which the adults sought" (Wallerstein and Kelly 1980, p. 313). The issues that are of crucial importance relate to the availability of supports for children and parents' ability to carefully make and implement plans. Respect for children's feelings and desires should not be translated into following their preferences about divorce. Children cannot make informed decisions about their own best interests; certainly they do not have the wisdom or altruism to assess the best interest of parents. Some children are angered by divorce or become co-opted or manipulated by one parent to oppose a separation. Often a child's caretaking concerns propel them to attempt to rescue the more needy or distressed parent. Wallerstein and Kelly (1980) report that many older adolescents report with shame and regret their vehement protests at the time of divorce, when they were younger and over-whelmed with fear and anger. At an older age, they can concur in the wisdom of the family's dissolution.

The greatest danger to children's future health and adjustment is disrupted parenting. Impoverished or erratic parent–child contact creates feelings of rejection and abandonment. Whether parents only threaten to withdraw or actually abandon their children temporarily or permanently, the result is narcissistic imbalance and deficits in the ego's capacity to cope. The symptoms that arise from such a blow to children's self-esteem are many, including addictions, delinquency, lying, rage, and hypochondriacal concerns (Mishne 1992). Losing a parent by death is devastating, but does not have the personalized impact that occurs, in cases of abandonment, when a child feels given up, put aside, left, or lost. The young child cannot fathom the depth of the emotional problems that caused the parents to abandon their child. Rather, children often blame themselves or consider themselves bad or lacking in value and worth because they could not sustain and retain their parents' commitment. The lack of finality in cases of abandonment feeds the fantasy of eventual return and reunion, which is stimulated by occasional contacts or presents at Christmas or on birthdays. Abandoned children persist in the quest for their lost parents; they are often inconsolable and are hostile to those parental figures who are available. They present cycles of rage rather than grief; they repeatedly reject the available parents' efforts in a vindictive determination to prove that no one can help (Mishne 1979).

During and after divorce, some parents can arrive at mutual understandings and arrangements that are in the children's best interests. Because of anger, bitterness, and sorrow, many others need professional help from counselors, divorce mediators, or child therapists. When divorcing parents face a bewildering array of tasks and challenges to put their and their children's lives in order, they may feel overwhelmed and incapable of making sound decisions. Often help is needed as the marriage declines and divorce looms. Professional help can provide support and advice about how to inform children of the pending familial changes. Many parents need assistance in sorting out issues of finances, child care, custody, and visitation. Later, many need help when they contemplate remarriage and the challenges of a blended family, when children from each spouse's former marriage are united in some part-time living arrangement. Parents need personal and often professional supports so as not to unload and burden their children with the tensions of post-divorce life, and the inevitable vicissitudes, created by financial issues, work pressures, child care, and subsequent romantic relationships. These stresses, if shared by parents, generally are overwhelming to children of any age, and push them to parent their parents, while robbing them of their childhood. Children are traumatized when forced to serve as parents, or therapists and confidants for their divorcing parents.

ESSENTIAL HOME-BASED STRATEGIES TO SUPPORT SUCCESS IN SCHOOL

School is often the place where the outward signs of children's distress over parental separation first appear. When children suffer loss because of a parent's death, such news elicits various responses. Generally there is an outpouring of empathy and helpful consideration; these aid children to assimilate various aspects of the loss and to function in the school. "The teacher's reactions to a child whose parents are or have been in the process of divorce are quite different from those to the child whose parent died" (Garber 1984, p. 197). In the case of divorce, there is generally a conspiracy of silence involving parents, children, peers, and teachers. There is a notion of respecting children's privacy, but often teachers are at a loss as to what to say. Some teachers experience overt and covert anger toward the parents. This anger may be displaced onto the children, particularly a newly aggressive and unruly youngster who is reacting to changes in the family. Parents may be apprehensive about sharing news of an impending or in-process divorce at school, from fear of prejudice and judgment towards themselves and their children. Dr. Benjamin Garber (1984) suggests that such parental fears are often justified and reports expectations by teachers that children's academic, social, and behavioral adjustment continue as usual. Also noted are impatient reactions from some teachers when youngsters daydream or fall behind in their work. Wallerstein and Kelly (1980), interviewing teachers as part of their research, similarly noted teachers' concerns and interest, but also recognized that teachers' psychological training and knowledge may be limited. "Many teachers . . . clearly had not understood that the changes in behavior seen in their children after separation were a result of the youngster's increased anxiety and tension" (ibid., p. 265). This research team described having a mixed experience with teachers. Some teachers were sensitive and supportive; others expected children's distress to be put aside during school hours. Despite such findings, these researchers recommended informing teachers of major changes in children's lives. Because of the frequency of divorce, some teachers need to defend themselves against the pain of their students by denying the profound impact of divorce on children. Many teachers experience their own tensions during parent–teacher conferences, when they are confronted by two sets of parents with or without new partners.

In addition to communication with teachers and appropriate guidance counselors, parents must sustain ongoing contact with school personnel to monitor the situation and to provide whatever supports seem appropriate to children's changing behavior and academic and social adjustment. The onset of change is unpredictable. Some children show an immediate reaction and decline; in others, the change is more gradual. Some children have a delayed response; others show distress at home but little at school. The wide range of reactions may be manifested by distractibility, endless requests for individual attention, lack of concentration, aggressiveness, withdrawal and daydreaming, sadness and depression, sudden social alienation due to strident, bossy behavior, bad temper and irritability, moodiness, rebellion toward teachers, and hypersensitivity to constructive criticism and instruction. Many, especially adolescents, act defiant, but youngsters whose social and academic achievements were previously good increased their school-related activities after parental separation (Wallerstein and Kelly 1980). Some children seemingly throw themselves into their schoolwork to blot out sadness and anger.

Children's responses in school appear to be "strongly linked to the custodial parents' continued ability to handle the children without serious deterioration and to protect the children from the divorce turmoil. It was additionally helpful if the other parent was able, as well, to be comforting and sensitive to the child's needs" (Wallerstein and Kelly 1984, p. 271). As can be expected, suffering and decline in school performance is most intense in situations where parental conflict continues unabated and where children feel, or indeed are, unprotected or misused by parents to do battle or to attempt parental reconciliation. Research findings underscore a mother's distress level as the most significant variable and one that affects her child's ability to learn. Because so much depends on mothers, the more common custodial parents, their well-being cannot be overestimated. It is important that mothers not berate themselves when they feel overcome and overwhelmed by one of life's greatest stressors. If the decision to divorce and the process of the divorce prove overwhelming, the best source of relief is generally professional therapy. Seeking help is not self-indulgent; it is a pressing necessity for parents and disrupted children. Such home-based intervention goes far in ameliorating the situation and reverberates in the school setting. Well-functioning children may use school for support and structure, but "fewer children than one had hoped really utilized or were capable of falling back upon the school network" (Wallerstein and Kelly 1984, p. 279).

During divorce and post-divorce adjustment, it is most important for parents to realize that expectations of schools and teachers must be realistically limited. Chil-

dren's adjustment and future course are strongly linked
to the family and extended family network; schools can
often do little to effect relief or to improve functioning.
Some schools have sophisticated and psychologically
trained teachers and pupil personnel services and staff.
These settings and individuals can provide compassionate understanding and tolerance for dramatic
changes and regression in a child. Nevertheless, they
cannot effect basic change in the child's self-esteem.
Many depressed and angry children spurn teachers' so-
licitude from frustration that it may not be forthcoming
in the home or from noncustodial parents. Dramatic
changes compared to children's earlier performances are
often linked to a sudden curtailment of contact with
fathers. Erratic and infrequent paternal visiting patterns
create a sense of devaluation and poor self-esteem.
Feeling defeated in maintaining a father's regular attention, many children develop a sense of futility about
trying; nothing seems to earn and sustain their father's
approval and consistent attention. Some children, caught
in the onslaught of a combative divorce, shut down and
become closed off from learning. Knowledge and awareness are experienced as dangerous; having been overex-
posed to parental rage and conflict, these children seek a
stance of knowing nothing. Other youngsters have no
energy available for learning; they are consumed with
acute, hyperalert monitoring of their parents and parental
attitudes. Some may experiment with substance abuse to
ward off depression; others become addicted to drugs or
alcohol. Studies reveal recent dramatic increase in adolescents' drug usage; reports of January 1994 suggest the

endemic proportions, similar to the devastating statistics of the 1960s.

Marital treatment is an intervention that has been well known and well utilized for decades. Divorce counseling and divorce mediation are newer professional offerings. Custody litigation, although proliferating today, should be undertaken only as a last resort, in extreme situations, and almost never without first consulting mental-health specialists. The danger is that the litigation will damage children and their relationships with both parents. It is important for parents to realize that custody, visitation, support and all matters pertaining to children are never permanent, but always subject to court review and modification. Thus, parents are not helplessly trapped by initial arrangements, and there is rarely a need for custody battle except in extreme situations.

Prompt procurement of appropriate consultation and services is often the wisest course, to ensure the best shared-parenting responses. Agencies that provide services for divorcing parents and children are numerous. Appropriate skilled professionals are to be found at the myriad social service agencies, family service agencies, and mental health clinics for those needing low fees scaled to family income. Many private practitioners, such as clinical social workers, psychologists, child psychiatrists, or child analysts, have significant experience and expertise in assessment and treatment of divorcing parents and their children. Referrals are often effectively made by school personnel, school-based clinicians, pediatricians, and clergymen.

The reason for seeking help before or during the divorce is to stave off regression. Professional treatment enables children of divorcing couples to receive prompt help so that problems are addressed quickly. If help is not received, problems may expand and youngsters may fall behind age-appropriate academic and social norms. Not being able to keep up academically and socially intensifies shame, guilt, and a sense of being different. When family life has failed, many children are ashamed before their peers; in addition they feel helpless, depressed, and angry about the events in the home. While parents are struggling with their own feelings, they are commonly aware of, and feel helpless about alleviating their child's pain. Predivorce parent guidance can help and is best done jointly with both partners. "Joint counseling gives the therapist the best opportunity to hear both spouses' opinions and thereby reduces the chance of a distorted view. In addition, it lessens the likelihood that the therapist will be seduced into taking sides" (Gardner 1979, p. 180). Joint interviews do not preclude individual and family interviews. Common questions posed are: "Should we get divorced, or stay together for the sake of the children?" "At what age is divorce more or less detrimental to a child?" "How do we explain divorce to our children?" Clearly, professionals must remain neutral. Assisting parents to clearly understand their situation helps them become equipped to make their own decisions. Guidance and counseling often continue during the divorce and the early postseparation period.

Specific parental responses have been part of the mythology of the divorce processes. None is more significant than the injunction to always reassure children that the noncustodial parent still loves them. It is not helpful to a child of any age to be told that an absent and/or neglectful parent still loves them. Parents have been misled about what is and is not psychologically devastating for a child. When a child is told that an abandoning and/or, abusive father "loves them," the mother is confusing the child about what is, and is not, loving behavior. A loving relationship must demonstrate loving and responsible behavior. Children who have been abandoned must come to terms with the reality parent and surrender the idealized, romanticized illusion. Additionally necessary for the child to work through and appreciate is the reality that the parent's failure to parent is not the result of some difficulty within the child, but rather lies with the parent.

Similarly, parents have been advised not to over-criticize an ex-spouse to the child, but this often breaks down, with such comments as: "I never criticize your father to you" or "There are many critical things I could say about your mother, but it's not right for me to tear her down" (Gardner 1979). Children need to know that parents divorced for real reasons, such as different views and values, and these differences should not be swept under the rug. When different views and conflictual areas are shared in anger with the child, these generally are distortions. When they are referred to realistically, in a manner that is age-appropriate for the child, the child is aware of substantial areas of disagreement and is not drawn into having to take sides. The child realizes that he or she will eventually need to sort out his or her priorities, and views of the two parents, as well as possible over time.

An example would be a mother's response when her ex-husband cancels visitation, supposedly from work pressures, for the third time in a month. She expresses impatience and annoyance; this is followed by her daughter Sally's protestations and defense of her father: "But Mom, he has to work. I can understand and I hope he'll come next week. Why do you always criticize and disapprove of him?" A reasoned, maternal answer would be as follows: "Sally, in my opinion, parents have responsibilities for children and work, and, I'll never be comfortable or casual when you and your brothers are always the last thing on your Dad's list of priorities. This is one of the many reasons your Dad and I couldn't continue to live together. We never could agree on how to share our work and family responsibilities. We are very different people with very different views and values, and we each balance things out in the ways we think best. You don't have to take sides or agree with me or him. We are who we are, and I'm sorry that we couldn't resolve things and keep the family together." Children in intact homes are also confronted with parental disagreements, but these differences are absorbed in the "good enough" home environment that embodies respect, affection, commitment, and rituals of intact family life.

The critical issue in the divorced home is what happens after the divorce. In the optimal situation quarreling and friction end, and children are not used as messengers of the conflict between eternally warring parents. Children can be comfortable and grow properly in a post-divorce home if they are provided a stable life with a minimum of friction between the parents and can enjoy adequate and consistent contact with approving and loving parents who provide freedom from economic worries. Children followed by research studies were found to have a good post-divorce outcome when both parents were able to restabilize and restore parenting after a disorienting transition period. Custodial and non-custodial parents of successful children did well in their respective separate lives and in cooperation with each other by retaining their commitments to their children. Divorce, though painful, is not devastating when *children* are not divorced from their parents. Many children derive additional benefits from parents' remarriage. Continuity of care, concern, and connection with *both* parents are the keys to successful outcomes at all ages.

12

Parenting Gone Awry: Good Intentions and Unintended Consequences

Flawed parental responses are universal and inevitable. No one can blame parents for their actions, attitudes, and mistakes. Instead it is important to attempt to identify causal sequences; parents' behaviors and personalities are determined by their background and what they did and did not receive from their parents (Kohut 1984). Because it is profitable to learn what to avoid in the future, recognition of mistakes must not be turned into a personal indictment, but rather seen as useful information. There is no value in mourning about what has gone wrong; mistakes are commonly made unwillingly and unconsciously. Any attempt to literally follow a cookbook of recipes for proper handling of problems is often detrimental and offers no solution; in such a procedure, the parents' responses can only be artificial and lacking ease and spontaneity. The correct approach can be found in many different ways, and it is important not to seek explicit answers and suggestions that may be restrictive or not easily or sensibly transferable to other, similar seeming situations.

It is helpful to learn the details of some erroneous approaches so as to stimulate consideration of maladaptive global patterns to know what to try to avoid. Dreikurs (1992) believes that all errors arise from three sources: "(1) The child is not required to observe order; (2) the parent allows himself to be drawn into conflict with the child; (3) the child is discouraged" (pp. 96–97). By trying to avoid conflict, some parents continuously give in and neglect to educate the child to social conformity, which requires the ability to wait and tolerate delay and frustration. At the opposite end of the continuum are parents who are bent on forcing their child to follow orders under all circumstances, an approach that inevitably leads to bitter struggles. René Spitz (1957) stated that frustration is a necessary requisite for the integration of the reality principle; thus it is as disastrous to bring up children with unqualified permissiveness as it is to have them encounter overwhelming frustration. The results of overgratification or massive frustration are distorted personality development. Spitz's research demonstrated the crucial importance of consistent empathic parenting that is characterized by attunement, limit–setting and parents' infinite pleasure and interest in the child.

It is critical that the parent–child relationship embody respect for mutual dignity. All mistakes seem to be due to various forms of violation of this fundamental principle. Parents who fail to respect their child will humiliate, enslave, frustrate, or overprotect them. Equally important are the consequences of parents' disregarding their own dignity. They will not earn the child's respect if the youngster bosses, ignores, or abuses them. No parent can enslave their child, or become enslaved by the child. Dr. Haim Ginott (1956) distinguishes between parental needs and children's tyranny. He notes that parents must love and like their children but "not have an urgent need to be liked by them every moment of the day" (ibid., p. 109). Parents who are fearful of losing their child's love dare not deny anything, even control of the home. Children are sensitive to their anxiety and exploit it mercilessly. They become tyrants who rule overanxious parental servants. In such situations, children may threaten parents with everything including withdrawing love. Because parents feel threatened, they cry and cajole their children and continually placate them by being overpermissive. Ideally, parents must distinguish between permissiveness and overpermissiveness. Permissiveness, literally defined, means permitting, in this case, children's age-appropriate wishes, needs, and behaviors, except for destructive and excessively aggressive behavior. The freedom to wish is absolute, but overpermissiveness is gratifying any and all wishes, including undesirable ones. Permissiveness brings confidence and increases children's capacity to express feelings and thoughts. Overpermissiveness brings anxiety and the escalation of unacceptable behaviors. It is important to distinguish between wishes and acts. It is the latter that generally require limiting.

Not only is there a great difference between older and newer approaches to discipline and child rearing, there appear to be cycles in the recommendations. In the early nineteenth century, often excessive strictness prevailed. By midcentury, a shift to demand feeling and greater permissiveness occurred, and excessive permissiveness often prevailed. Currently the emphasis is on attempting to help children with both feelings and conduct. When restrictions are imposed, they must be applied without malice or excessive anger. Parents ideally empathize with children, even with their resentments, when limited. Limits must be applied in a manner that preserves children's and parents' self-respect; thus limits must not be arbitrary or capricious. Children are "not punished additionally for not liking prohibitions" (Ginott 1956, p. 113). Children need clear distinctions between acceptable and unacceptable behavior, and in the absence of limits, they experience anxiety at not being stopped or not knowing how far they can go. Certain behaviors are sanctioned and approved of; others are not sanctioned but temporarily tolerated because of special stress situations like illness, divorce, or death in the family; and others cannot be tolerated at all. Limits should be phrased concisely, even impersonally, in a lang iage that does not challenge children's self-respect and allows them to respond positively. Endless lectures and explanations often tell children that parents are uncertain and are trying to convince themselves as well as their children.

SPOILING THE CHILD

It is not easy to accurately define what we mean by "spoiling" a child since this includes a great variety of attitudes and actions, but the end result is that the child is not trained to meet the responsibilities of living, that he or she has been "spoiled" for these duties and rendered unfit to perform them. An example is Gil, who has never been expected to clean up after himself or put his room and possessions in order. His counselor at overnight camp sarcastically told Gil's parents that they should have sent him to camp with a maid and that Gil did his part only under severe peer-group coercion. His cabinmates were furious at him because Gil's sloppy area caused the bunk as a whole to get demerits. Years later at college, Gil's inability to order himself and his things continues to have significant, indeed serious, ramifications. He is in a continual frenzied search for classnotes, research cards, notebooks, and papers written. He has been "spoiled" and rendered unfit for age-appropriate academic mastery, care of himself and his belongings, and management of time and money.

Commonly, spoiling children arises out of well-intentioned parental efforts to spare them unpleasant experiences or the drudgery of daily living. Because some parents are overly concerned with or overly attached to their children, they never frustrate them or insist on enforcement of any order. Parents may succumb to spoiling and pampering an only child, one who has suffered any significant illness, or one who is exceptionally attractive or bright. Such pampering assumes "a thousand different forms. The child grows up in a hothouse atmosphere in which the natural order that otherwise regulates human conduct is not in force. He is beyond the jurisdictions of (rules and expectations) that bind the other members of the household" (Dreikurs 1992, p. 100).

A spoiled and overprotected child is shrouded in excessive layers of tenderness, affection, sympathy, and overindulgence such that he or she is consistently shielded from the consequences of his actions. The child's every wish is catered to, and the child always gets his or her own way despite the inconvenience to others in the family. Such children will not learn how to subordinate their desires to others, and, contrary to parents' expectations, they are not especially happy. Others can expect and surmount rebuffs or obstacles on the course toward achievement, but the pampered child generally cannot persevere and often feels ignored or ill-treated when not at center stage. "The discontent, impatience and joylessness that characterizes so many spoiled children shows to what little extent spoiling has succeeded in making life easier for them" (Dreikurs 1992, p. 101). Inevitably such spoiling and pampering lead to parent–child conflict. There is an end to what parents can in fact do for their children. Children find it almost impossible to understand why they must suddenly do without the accustomed amount of help and overindulgence that has always been provided. Spoiling commonly produces a turbulent cycle of severity and laxity, affection and anger, and mutually shared desperation. The basis of spoiling children generally emanates from parents' response to their own anxiety and need for excessive attachment, rather than from a sound appraisal of their children's age-appropriate ability and readiness for greater independence. Parental anxiety propels overprotectiveness and excessive holding onto children. The

overassumption of a child's responsibilities often occurs·
in the realm of school.

Ramifications that Create Educational Problems

When parents spoil and pamper, they infantilize children
in the area of learning and academic performance. Parents
may do more homework than the child does. They may
allow the child to procrastinate over homework or to do
a sloppy, incomplete, last-minute job while watching
television, talking on the phone, or listening to a full-
blast stereo. Some parents rush about, going to the library for their child, doing the required research
themselves. They may allow the child to have an excess
of extracurricular activities and attend to homework afterward. They accept children's arguments about when
they will do their homework, and their complaints, procrastination, and excuses that continue until bedtime.
When homework ranks last after gymnastic classes,
sporting events, and socializing, overindulgent parents
permit these erroneous priorities. Because they want
their child to be popular, athletic, and not engaged in
battle with them, they condone homework that is raced
through, even if the result is incorrect, messy, or incomplete. "Forgetters frequently fail to remember to bring
work home or forget that they have homework at all"
(Canter and Hausner 1987, p. 27). Some overly solicitous
parents cover for their children by sending excuse notes
or allowing them to stay home to avoid a quiz or test they
are not prepared for.

Vignette

The aforementioned Gil, a bright, tall, blonde, very
attractive only child, suffered major learning problems
and academic anxiety. His parents, an affluent Catholic
couple, continuously attempted to spare him the pain
and struggle involved in learning and mastery. They
would change schools to place him in less demanding
settings, do his homework for him, purchase Cliff's
Notes, handle return of library brooks, and be amused
that he used and re-used one book report throughout
high school. Problems began in the earliest grades,
when play preceded homework time. The results have
been disastrous, with lifelong poor self-esteem, exam
anxiety, and a total absence of confidence in his own
efforts. Gil repeatedly failed at two private schools
until he was asked to leave. Therapy over an extended
period for child and parents has been necessary to
enable Gil to finally enter a special college program.
Despite an undemanding course of study, he struggles
with shaky study skills and major time management
problems created by the constant avoidance of daily
study. He is slowly succeeding in surmounting his
patterns of "forgetting" assignments, or of last-
minute racing through projects and papers, both of
which result only in incomplete or superficial productions. Panic and exam anxiety are lessened, and for the
first time in his life Gil has achieved above-average
grades. Therapy has succeeded in separating Gil from
his parents in handling his work and formulating realistic goals and aspirations. Therapy has also stimulated

in him a belated but gradually evolving intellectual curiosity and interest in learning. Gil's joy over two final A grades, his first ever, was enormous in the sophomore year of college.

DYSFUNCTIONAL PARENTHOOD: ABUSE AND NEGLECT

Dreikurs (1992) acknowledges that parents who really dislike their children are an exception today. Child abuse and child neglect nevertheless occur for myriad reasons, most frequently when parents themselves were abused or neglected. An atmosphere of lovelessness or a cyclical pattern of affection alternating with aggression or neglect inevitably creates a wretched, hostile, and defiant child. Planned parenthood may reduce the number of unwanted children, but in today's world, the rise in unmarried-teen pregnancies is astronomical. When children feel rejected and unloved or are actually abandoned, they are permanently crippled. Because child maltreatment is on the rise, many children require placement out of the home, with relatives or in foster care. "Yearly estimates of the number of abused and neglected children vary from one-half million to as many as four million" (Gonzalez-Ramos and Goldstein 1989, p. 3).

Since the early 1960s, greater awareness and study of child maltreatment has been stimulated by the work of Dr. Henry Kempe, who was the first to coin the phrase *battered child*. There are many definitions of child maltreatment in the literature. The concept includes abuse (when parents or caretakers inflict or permit injury or protracted impairment of emotional or physical health) and neglect (when physical, mental, or emotional condition is impaired or at risk of impairment as a result of parents' failing to provide adequate basic care and supervision). Sexual abuse, which often accompanies physical abuse, involves committing sexual offenses or allowing such offenses to be committed upon children.

There is no agreed-upon single explanation for child maltreatment; a "complex interaction of biological, psychological, environmental and societal factors occurs in most cases" (Gonzalez-Ramos and Goldstein 1989, p. 6). Common determinants are the parents' history and characteristics, children's temperament and characteristics, early parent–child relationships, and environmental and familial stressors such as illness, unemployment, substance abuse, and domestic violence. A frequent though not universal finding is that parents who were abused in their youth commonly abuse their children. Such parents may relive their own childhood in the process of parenting (Benedek 1959). Abusive parents suffer poor self-esteem and undeveloped or poorly developed coping capacities; they are easily vulnerable to stress and frustration in their parenting roles and tasks. These parents lack empathy for their children and instead identify with their own abusive parents. Many of these parents are apathetic, overwhelmed, or hopeless. They are plagued with emotional numbness and inhibition, which periodically erupt into out-of-control desperation, rage, and impulsive actions. Children appear at high risk for maltreatment if they were unplanned and unwanted, the wrong sex, or the perfect replica of a hated partner. Parents may also mistreat children with temperament problems like hyperactivity, fussiness, irregular sleep patterns or incessant arguing.

Parental and child characteristics often are a misfit, whereby a dynamic interchange occurs, with spiral effects, in which an abused child counters with aggressive and provocative acts which incite the parent, eliciting more and more potential for harm. Child abuse is all too common in impoverished female-headed homes, where overwhelmed mothers and/or their impermanent partners may take out their frustrations on the available scapegoats, the children. Although it abounds in hazardous, impoverished environments, child abuse is found among all socioeconomic and ethnic groups. Child maltreatment cannot be equated with parent's deliberate and willful malevolence. Instead, it is an intergenerationally transmitted pattern that requires communal and professional intervention to stop the cycle.

The characteristics of these child victims are varied but specific patterns are common, such as a proneness to action without any thought as to social expectations, property, safety, or consideration for the feelings of others. They are frequently labeled hyperactive, which is an appropriate adjective but all too often an inappropriate diagnosis; that is, they are often medicated as though they were suffering from what is now called *attention deficit disorder* (Burland 1984). These words, too, "are *descriptively* accurate, but medication is ineffective in this syndrome except for its placebo effect upon parents and teachers" (Burland 1984, p. 148). Abused children have never participated in the "dialogue" between child and mother, the communication and bonding process extensively studied by Brazelton and colleagues (Brazelton 1981, Brazelton and Als 1979). These children showed various degrees of early failure to thrive and were fussy, inconsolable, limp, and lost-appearing. They begin their first year of life unrelated and remain so, with dire consequences for affective and cognitive development. Early on, primitive destructive aggression appears and continues; and because there is an absence of close, loving ties they cannot learn to love, in the absence of consistent love. Lack of socialization skills and explosive rage reactions are common.

Ramifications that Create Educational Problems

Devoid of basic trust, abused children cannot enter into any school program with an ability to appropriately relate or respond to peers or teachers. They often feel real only when experiencing instant gratification, when being destructive, or when convinced by their own wishes and illusions of grandiosity, which cover a core of fear, loneliness, and depression. J. Alexis Burland (1984) notes an ongoing cycle of wild, incoherent, destructive, and self-destructive behaviors. Along with behavior characteristics are innumerable cognitive deficits. Interpersonal, behavioral, and academic problems are enormous.

All such parent–child dyads require professional or communal intervention, or both. Parents often are compelled to become nonvoluntary clients. Some situations are amenable to psychotherapy and do not require out-of-home placement. In such dysfunctional homes, children's adolescence is always turbulent and difficult.

> Those mothers, marginal but not altogether inadequate, who do better, do so primarily because some spark of maternal empathic relatedness is kindled, sometimes by the child, sometimes by a sensitive counselor who can activate in the therapeutic relationship the tenderness needed for parenting. Almost like magic this spark brings life to the child, the mother, the dyad and the counselor. [Burland 1984, p. 160]

Treatment plans and strategies must be aimed at what is referred to as the "subculture of parental deprivation." Home-focused interventions are the only way to make a difference for such damaged youth, who are commonly contained in small special education classes in public schools or in therapeutic day and residential schools.

Vignette

Ms. C, a beautiful 33-year-old African-American single parent on public assistance, was referred by the school to an urban child-guidance clinic for an evaluation of her 9-year-old daughter, Mary. Mary did no work in school, refused to talk or respond appropriately to peers or her teacher, and on numerous occasions had wild temper tantrums in class and on the playground. Ms. C acknowledged being in a frenzy over her daughter, who was late to school almost daily

because she refused to leave her mother and the playground to enter the building. She played with matches,
swore, and was generally noncommunicative except in
impulsive, angry outbursts. Ms. C described her state
of agitation and her futile attempts to discipline and
scold her daughter and make her do her homework.
She often whipped Mary in desperate attempts to make
her comply and cooperate. In answer to the therapist's
questions and history taking, she revealed her own
fears of inadequacy and her apprehension that Mary
might be taken away from her. Ms. C had been re-
moved from her home and had spent her childhood in
an oppressive, rigid children's institution, and she
feared the same for her child.

Once the mother found she could relax in an unthrea-
tening and supportive atmosphere, she proved to be open
and accessible. Without any threat of losing her child, or
being judged badly, she was heartened by the worker's
respect for her concerns and understanding attitude
about the origin of her excessive physical discipline and
reassurances that soon, more effective parenting skills
would be discussed and shared in their ongoing contact.
[Mishne 1989, p. 47]

EXCESSIVE ANXIETY

Anxious parents often see endless dangers from which
they wish to shield their children. Most children who are
endlessly hovered over become resentful and excessive in
risk taking. Deprived of valuable learning experiences,
they fulfill their parents' worst apprehensions. Their

antagonism at endless accounts of their parents' fears and at lectures on safety causes them to rebel. In some cases, they submit and adopt squeamish, timid notions from their parents. Submission, rebellion, or a combination of both as responses to parental anxiety do not enable children to mature or have adequate self-esteem. Rather, they become anxious themselves.

> It is strange but true that excessive caution leads to the same results as thoughtlessness. Anticipating dangers not only causes hesitancy, but actually drives people headlong into the very dangers they wish to avoid. The evasion of risks requires calm presence of mind and a clear appraisal of the situation. Hence, over-rating danger is equivalent to increasing it. [Dreikurs 1992, pp. 109–110]

Sound judgment is better than anxiety as a preventive against danger. When parents attempt to share their fears and intimidate their child, they are putting them in harm's way. Hovering over children and bundling them up excessively almost predestines these youngsters to be sickly.

Extreme anxiety often is manifested by oversupervision, which interferes with children's making their own decisions and behaving with confident independence. Parents can exhaust themselves and their children in an endless torrent of directives when they relentlessly overmanage them. Every action and activity is overseen, and the parents' running comments and prohibitions continue unabated. Not an hour or a day is free of exhortations and expression of parental opinions. What anxious parents commonly fail to realize is that despite good intentions, they are driving children away. When exhaustion prevails, children turn an increasingly deaf ear to parents. They stop paying attention when they feel badgered and harangued at. They may adopt inappropriate, rebellious behavior or submit in a sullen and unresponsive fashion.

Excessive talking often signifies extreme parental anxiety. The torrent of words, however, is often experienced as intrusive and offensive, and it may generate antagonism. Repetitive litanies, discussions, prohibitions, and directions commonly backfire and spark unpleasant bickering. Silence is too frequently unrecognized by parents as one of the most eloquent sounds. Silence generally succeeds and is preferable to endless accountings of mistakes made. Parents' words should ideally be stimulating and supportive, not annoying and critical, but excessive talking often becomes nagging and harping. "The very incessancy of the practice, combined with a poverty of inventive imagination, leads to a monotonous reiteration of the same phases" (Dreikurs 1992, pp. 124–125). Children who are always told what to do may comply, be polite, keep a tidy room, and so on, but nevertheless make irresponsible decisions. If children are deprived of the opportunity to exercise judgments and make choices, they rarely develop confidence or inner standards.

Ginott (1956) cautions that in instances of declared and undeclared war in the home over chores and the like, parents cannot win the war. "Children have more time and energy to resist us than we have to coerce them" (ibid., p. 84). Even when parents win the battle, they generally lose the war. Children may retaliate by becoming spiritless and depressed or defiant and rebellious. The only way to win is by winning children over by listening with sensitivity and respect, not by badgering them with words, threats, accusations, and criticisms that create hatred and resentment. Parents must state their feelings, thoughts, and wishes without attacking or insulting the child. Badgering children with incessant talk, advice, and warnings is experienced as belittling and insulting. Only an emphatic stance and sympathetic atmosphere engage them, and ultimately they respond to civility, fairness, and reason.

Parents must distinguish between fault finding or berating children and offering correction and instruction. Disparagement and fault finding are forms of one-upmanship. Rendered in a harsh and reproachful tone, they tend to discourage children to such a degree that they abandon their efforts and refuse to try. Friendly persuasion, encouragement, and correction set a better tone and demonstrate that children need not give up persevering. Many children feel that parental standards are excessive, anxiety riddled, and perfectionistic. No matter how hard they try, they never can do a thing that pleases their parents. Disparagement over grades, weight, bad habits like nail-biting, and so on generally stimulates continuation of the very thing parents want their children to change. Children who feel insulted or humiliated become defiant and offer resistance.

Disparagement or severity hampers any sense of well-being and causes a child to feel helpless, weak, and dependent. If parents, out of excessive anxiety are extremely dominating or given to mortifying the child in an effort to extract obedience, the child will be crippled and unable to function autonomously. Most offensive is any physical punishment. When some parents defend or justify physical punishment, they are seemingly unaware that they have identified with their own parents and are out of touch with their child, or themselves in their earlier years, when they were forced to submit to spankings or whippings. *No genuine impulse toward good behavior emerges out of physical punishment.* "On the contrary, there is every reason to expect that the child will deteriorate further; and even the most savage blows can have no beneficial effect on his attitude. His inner resistance is not broken, but fortified by whipping" (Dreikurs 1992, p. 135). If children have been exposed only to physical punishment, this becomes the only thing that will make them obey, and in fact they often deliberately provoke punishment. This ominous pattern creates a desire for punishment and a pathological excitement and attachment to brutality. Every person who was beaten as a child shows the marks in his or her character and commonly in his or her own subsequent parenting patterns. Brutality, hardness, and harshness are inevitable outcomes of corporal childhood discipline. What is unrecognized or overlooked is the cowardice implicit in such a parental approach, easily recognized when an older child bullies a smaller and younger child. "The individual who was humbled and repressed as a child is never a real social being; he remains a half-tamed animal. Therefore, a method of training that aims to make the child an active member of society must avoid any expedient that tends to suppress and humiliate him" (Dreikurs 1992, p. 140).

Ramifications that Create Educational Problems

Overanxious parents convey their worries and excessive fears in a multitude of ways, such as hovering over or infantilizing their children and offering them endless cautions and warnings. They may express their feelings with barrages of talk, advice, and direction, with coercion, nagging, faultfinding, and swearing, and even with physical punishment. All of these actions are parent-centered, not child-centered, and generally reflect a parent's excessive concerns, need for over-control, and fears of the child's separateness and autonomy. The parents, out of anxiety, cannot contain their need to demonstrate power and superiority. Only an unconscious sense of impotence and helplessness can compel a parent to raise a hand against a child. All of these parental attitudes and actions are predicated on the idiom that the parent must remain in charge. This is at cross purposes to the socialization and learning process of children of all ages.

Learning, academics, social skills, and sports must be the child's responsibility. These tasks must be transacted between child, teacher, and peers, and if the parent holds on anxiously and punitively, the child and parent are never free from bondage. Schoolwork and social interactions become the child's secret unconscious weapon, with which to punish, blackmail, or exploit the parents. If children have been denied responsibility for decision making, independent work, and inner-directed self-control, they will continue to overly rely on others to endlessly supervise, decide, evaluate, and punish them. They will not enter into the struggle to master complex ideas, but will feel defeated before they start or helpless to handle a task in a fashion that does not evoke criticism and complaint. Many capable children lag in their academic achievement as an unconscious rebellion against parental anxiety, pressure, and ambitions. To succeed independently requires achieving a sense of individuality and age-appropriate separateness from excessive closeness to the parents. Anxious and demanding parents who are too emotionally involved in their child's performance interfere with the child's assumption of responsibility. "If homework and high grades become diamonds in his parents' crown, the child may unconsciously prefer to bring home a crown of weeds that at least is his own" (Ginott 1956, p. 93).

Children cannot feel that they are evaluated only for their productions and achievements and not for themselves. Feeling that they are nothing but a narcissistic extension or mirror for the parents' aspirations causes children to flounder, hesitate, and ultimately rebel. "They can take away the TV and the allowance but they cannot take away my failing grades" (Ginott 1956, pp. 93–94). Resistance to studying is not a simple problem solved by toughness or leniency. Increased pressure may increase a child's resistance, and a laissez-faire stance may suggest parental acceptance of immaturity and irresponsibility. Each situation requires an individual assessment. Solutions will generally not be quick or easy. Consultation with teachers is a necessary first step, and in many in-

stances, parents and child might need outside professional help. A self-aware parent may recognize but not be
able to contain excessive anxiety, criticism, hovering,
and nagging. An older child may be aware of exam
anxiety and concentration problems but be at a total loss
to correct these problems or alter long-standing patterns
of procrastination and avoidance of homework and
study.

Vignette

When Mike was ten years old, the school psychologist
and school social worker referred him and his parents
to a child psychiatry clinic for a fuller evaluation and
for therapy. Mike, from a working class African-
American family was described as a very bright child
who read far above grade level but refused to produce
in school. He refused to participate in class discussions,
or interact with peers, and the school planned to fail
him on the basis of his refusal to work. Mike had to be
prodded to get up, dress, and depart for school. He
dawdled constantly and provoked parents and teachers
continuously. They all confessed to exploding and
repeatedly spanking him severely. He was so infuriating that even the clinic psychologist ruefully acknowledged yelling at and scolding him during the
testing process. Not asked to produce or submit to
tests in therapy sessions, Mike was neither provocative
nor passive-aggressive in his relationship with his
therapist. In therapy sessions he was verbal and artic-

ulate and spent much time drawing and sharing fantasies and wishes. He was able to share his concerns
about his angry impulses, initially experienced as fears
of fires, floods, and storms. He did endless drawings of
airplanes, racing cars, and ships, and gradually shared
his megalomaniac and grandiose fantasies through the
epics and stories he thought up to accompany his
drawings.

Mike made significant gains in response to two years
of therapy and his parents' improved handling of him.
The parents were responsive to parent guidance and
realizing that they were not alone in their concern
about Mike, were able to completely and permanently
curtail all physical punishment or explosive anger.
They became more tolerant, relaxed, and nonreactive
to Mike's provocativeness, and he was then able to
surrender this behavior, since his parents no longer
were incitable. Mike's schoolwork improved enor-
mously and he achieved at a superior level commensurate with his intellectual capacities. As he surrendered
his provocativeness at home, so did he at school. He
began to participate in swimming classes and a Little
League baseball team. Buoyed by improved self-
esteem, his peer interactions slowly increased and improved. Mike was increasingly able to verbalize
feelings and fantasies rather than confining them to his
solitary daydreaming and drawing. He was able to
articulate that treatment helped him figure things out:

. . . like my imagination baby games and heroes, full of
monsters, racing cars, rock stars and pilots. I used to lose

myself thinking about those make-believe people because I'm the opposite, and want to feel good and forget I'm the shortest in my class, not popular, not a big shot, not a great athlete, and too frightened to fight and defend myself. I'm now an excellent student and it's the only thing in my control. I guess I'm just brains and not brawn.

As Mike's treatment continued, he was able to get to the early significant trauma of his early years, the shocking death of his grandmother, his primary caretaker for his first five years of life, due to his parents' work schedules. When he was able to mourn this loss and associate the unexpected trauma with his fears of other unexpected, destructive phenomena like floods, lightening, and thunder, his fears diminished and he increasingly entered the world of his peers with greater confidence and competence. At the conclusion of his therapy, he had better realized the hopes and aspirations of his earlier fantasies and daydreams. Not only was he a fine student, but with time and treatment, he relaxed, succeeded in sports and athletics, and became a respected, well-liked, more popular member of his group. Though cautious with his peers and at times a bit standoffish, Mike made significant gains in his capacity to form friendships. His relationships with his parents, teachers, and siblings improved dramatically. His pubescent growth spurt and physical and emotional maturation secured his improved sense of self and gave him more solid self-esteem (Mishne 1983).

13

Summary
and Conclusions

Parenthood refers to the choice to become a parent as well as to the kind of parent one becomes. Attitudes about parenthood and toward children have changed many times throughout history, and the state of flux continues. Despite the changing perspectives,

> Parents have been the subject of universal interest since the beginning of time. Although they represent the origin of us all, their position vis-à-vis their offspring was always so tenuous that the fifth commandment in the Bible states especially to "Honor thy father and thy mother as the Lord thy God commanded thee." [Offer 1984a, p. xiii]

Some researchers have viewed parenthood from a developmental perspective. They extend their observations to the entire life cycle and study not only the parents of young children, but also the tasks and roles of school-age children, adolescents, and young adults. As children grow older, the family faces inevitable vicissitudes in the child–parent relationship when offspring struggle for their own separate identity (Benedek 1959). Parenting is very hard work, but for those who succeed, the rewards are great. Failure results "in anxiety, frustration, friction, and perhaps shame or guilt may be severe" (Bowlby 1984, p. 269).

Erikson (1959) was the first theoretician to postulate life crisis throughout the life span. The fifth stage, adolescence, is one of *ego identity versus role diffusion.* Children finish high school, enter college, and struggle to define themselves in order to move into the sixth stage, *intimacy versus isolation,* when commitments are made to career or vocation and to enduring relationships with others. These stages of children's development coincide with Erikson's seventh stage, that of the parents, who struggle with *generativity versus stagnation*—a time of life when parents are engaged in establishing ties and guiding the next generation. They can find generativity not only in relation with their children but also in other interpersonal relationships. The essential ingredient in the gaining of a feeling of generativity involves an identification with the future, namely, the next generation.

Parents are universally viewed as the child's first teachers. Almost immediately they influence their child's behavior in one direction or another, and the range of techniques is vast. While some are restrictive and "certainly have a disciplinary intent, many of them are of an encouraging sort" (Erikson 1959, p. 277). John Bowlby (1984), an eminent child specialist, believes that provision of a secure life-long base, is the central feature of parenting. Such a base allows children a sense of security in making sorties to the outside world. They are completely confident that they can return and be welcomed, nourished physically and emotionally, comforted if distressed, and reassured if frightened. The major parenting role is thus defined as being available and responsive when called upon, ready to provide encouragement and assistance, and to intervene actively as necessary. Abundant research studies demonstrate that the most secure and successful children, who can make the most out of educational experiences and other opportunities, are those whose parents encouraged autonomy, but additionally were always available and responsive when needed. This availability does not end at adolescence, or at young adulthood, but rather must be sustained lifelong.

The demands of home and work create inordinate strains in maintaining optimal availability and responsiveness. Recent social changes have presented mothers with new options, especially for the middle class, in acquiring advanced education and securing choice positions. Successful professional women, mostly educated in the 1970s, once believed that they could combine high-powered careers with the family life they wanted. Recent interviews with such women (Apter 1993, Harrington 1992) revealed that many of them discovered that they did not want their careers after all or that they could not have careers if they wanted families as well. Many have opted out of the fast-track career route and surrendered the pressures of a corporation or a competitive law firm for less stressful work lives in smaller companies and law firms, to ensure life after work. Some men have made similar choices for the same reasons, but women far outnumber men in making this shift.

Working-class women have fewer choices and less education. They are commonly the most stressed parent population; they must contend with an often taxing and ungratifying job, financial pressures, and the demands of the home.

Until very recently, most examinations of parenthood focused almost exclusively on mothers, rather than on fathers as well. Early studies about fatherhood focused on father absence, with little attention paid to the positive and negative impact when fathers are present (Ross 1984). More recent studies of fatherhood (Demos 1982) note a discouraging trend, that of the gradual disengagement of men from home and family. Fathers rarely work at or near home.

> Advancing technology, occupational specialization and the vastness and complexity of the current economy have dealt successive death blows to the viability of the family as an essential socioeconomic unit. With this, a man's loyalties have shifted to his corporation or institution as the owner of his life, well-being and energies, indeed, his real family. [Ross 1984, p. 383]

Feeling abandoned, some wives have responded by their own disengagement from the family. They view work achievement as more fulfilling and creative than parenting and homemaking. Contemporary financial pressures exacerbate these role changes as well as the dissolution of family bonds. With exceptions here and there, studies suggest that husbands of working wives have not opted for coequal homemaking or child rearing. Parents must now face the consequences of latchkey

children and substandard day care in America. New legislation such as the Family and Medical Leave Act sets a
good precedent, but more changes in employment patterns and legislation for family supports are clearly necessary. If fathers and mothers are to parent, concerted
local and national efforts must be made to "lobby for the
time (and monies) necessary to do so. Quality is at least
partially a function of quantity" (Ross 1984, p. 384).

In addition to the stresses from the external world are
the personal and interpersonal ones. Extensive research
evidence demonstrates that parents' feelings and behaviors towards their children are deeply influenced by their
previous personal experiences and how they were paren-
ted. Some of the clearest evidence of the enormous part
played by childhood experiences in the way parents treat
children comes from studies of child abuse and emotional
neglect. Less-extreme maladaptive parenting is also
viewed as an intergenerationally transmitted pattern. In
spite of one's best intentions, parents commonly (not
uniformly) repeat their past in their parenting efforts. In
all, parents consciously do their best to raise and educate
their children effectively, yet despite their efforts, frequently their problems are generational ones, whereby
dysfunctional patterns are unconsciously passed on and
create successions of unfavorable parental attitudes and
behaviors. These unfavorable attitudes and patterns include excessive anxiety, overprotectiveness, overpermissiveness, and severity. Parents can take steps to undo
these problematic attitudes and behaviors and often can
best learn from example by attending parenting classes
and self-help groups. In some situations this suffices; in

others, individual or family treatment is indicated. Seeking help to parent more effectually is not a sign of failure. Rather, it is the result of honest self-appraisal and the motivation to try to do better in the centralmost significant role in adult life. Examination of one's parenting strengths and weaknesses provides a "connection of past experiences, present sources of satisfaction and dissatisfaction, and future intentions, hopes and fears" (Cohen et al. 1984, p. 398).

Understanding their personal and emotional history enhances people's capacity for parenting. Parents generally give insufficient attention to their own past experiences. The accumulation of these experiences and feelings has been either forgotten, repressed, or not recalled in words. Yet parents often behave toward their children as their parents behaved toward them. Some families are restrained, silent, strict, with an absence of communication and empathy from one generation to the next. "Each child is left to traverse life's problems alone, as though his responses were so unique and uncharacteristic that they must be kept private" (Paul 1970, p. 343). Before a parent can empathize with his or her child, they commonly have to develop or experience empathy for themselves. Empathy and flexibility permit the corresponding readjustment in parents' attitudes and behavior in response to the growing child's changing developmental needs.

One of the most salient features of American culture has been the all-too-frequent disengagement of fathers from active parenting and from the help-seeking process when this is necessary for child, family life, or both. American culture has been characterized as one of paternal deprivation. Despite the rapid increase in numbers of working mothers, in terms of parenting, the Momism of the '50s is still very much in the air (Ross 1984) as fathers continue to relegate responsibility for children to mothers. In contemporary society and with the increase of dual-career households, it appears that parental functions will not continue to be assigned along gender lines. "The notion of mothering or fathering may become passé and be replaced by the more important emphasis on mirroring" (Muslin 1984, p. 323), "sharing the inner mental life of the child, and witnessing the child's growth with joy" (ibid.). Fatherhood is belatedly being rediscovered as governmental agencies contemplate strategies and programs to keep families together to combat youth violence and adolescent acting-out behaviors.

Ideally, parenthood involves discipline of children, self-discipline, flexibility, and empathy by both parents. This is a difficult but not impossible achievement, despite the numerous cases of divorce. Additionally needed is commitment, one of the hardest ingredients of all, in the parenting process. Refusal to give up is exactly what parents attempt to teach their children. Learning to give up easily is a road to failure. Parents who do not want their children to fail cannot afford to give up on them. They may have to disengage, loosen the reins, and in some cases seek professional helpers, but their continued perseverance and commitment ensure children's sense of worth and willingness to trust themselves and others.

References

Apter, T. (1993). *Working Women Don't Have Wives: Professional Success in the 1990s.* New York: St. Martin's Press.

Arnstein, R. L. (1984). Young adulthood: stages of maturity. In *Normality and the Life Cycle: A Critical Integration,* ed. D. Offer and M. Sabshin, pp. 108–144. New York: Basic Books.

Baldwin, R. (1989). *You Are Your Child's First Teacher.* Berkeley, CA: Celestial Arts.

Balter, L. (1983). The technique of psychoanalytically oriented parent education. In *Ego and Self Psychology: Group Intervention with Children, Adolescents, and Parents,* ed. E. Buchholz and J. Mishne, pp. 57–64. New York: Jason Aronson.

Basch, M. (1983). Empathic understanding: a view of the concept of some theoretical considerations. *Journal of the American Psychoanalytic Association* 31:101–127.

Benedek, T. (1959). Parenthood as a developmental phase: a contribution to libido theory. *Journal of the American Psychoanalytic Association* 7:389–417.

_____ (1970). Parenthood during the life cycle. In *Parenthood: Its Psychology and Psychopathology,* ed. E. J. Anthony and T. Benedek. Boston: Little, Brown & Co.

Bettelheim, B. (1976). *The Uses of Enchantment.* New York: Knopf.

Blos, P. (1962). *On Adolescence.* New York: Free Press.

Bowlby, J. (1984). Caring for the young: influences on development. In *Parenthood: A Psychodynamic Perspective,* ed. R. S. Cohen, B. J. Cohler, and S. H. Weisman, pp. 373–390. New York: Guilford.

Brazelton, T. B. (1981). *The first four developmental stages in attachment of parent and infant.* Paper delivered at the twelfth annual Margaret S. Mahler Symposium, Philadelphia, May 1981.

Brazelton, T. B., and Als, H. (1979). Four early stages in the development of mother/infant interaction. In *Psychoanalytic Study of the Child* 34:349–370. New Haven, CT: Yale University Press.

Burland, A. (1984). Dysfunctional parenthood in a deprived population. In *Parenthood: A Psychodynamic Perspective,* ed. R. Cohen, B. J. Cohler, and S. H. Weisman, pp. 148–163. New York: Guilford.

Buxbaum, E. (1980). Between the Oedipus complex and adolescence: the "quiet" time. In *The Course of Life: Psychoanalytic Contributions to Understanding Personality Development, vol. 2: Latency, Adolescence and Youth,* ed. S. I. Greenspan and G. H. Pollock. Bethesda, MD: National Institute of Mental Health.

Canter, L., and Hausner, L. (1987). *Homework without Tears: A Parent's Guide for Motivating Children to Do Homework and to Succeed in School.* New York: Harper Perennial.

Chodorow, N. (1978). *The Reproduction of Mothering: Psychoanalysis and the Sociology of Gender.* Berkeley and Los Angeles: University of California Press.

Cohen, R. S., Cohler, B. J., and Weisman, S. H. (1984). *Parenthood: A Psychodynamic Perspective.* New York: Guilford.

Cohler, B. J., and Boxer, A. M. (1984). Middle adulthood: settling into the world—person, time and context. In *Normality and the Life Cycle: A Critical Integration,* ed. D. Offer and M. Sabshin, pp. 145–203. New York: Basic Books.

Cohn, S. J. (1988). Assessing the gifted child and adolescent. In *Handbook of Clinical Assessment of Children and Adolescents, Vol. 1,* ed. C. J. Kestenbaum and D. T. Williams, pp. 355–376. New York: New York University Press.

Demos, J. (1980). The changing face of fatherhood. In *Father and Child: Developmental and Clinical Perspectives,* ed. S. Cath, A. Guritt, and J. Ross, pp. 425–445. New York: Basil Blackwell.

Dizenus, I. M. (1979). Children and divorce. In *The Basic Handbook of Child Psychiatry,* ed. J. D. Noshpitz, J. D. Call, R. L. Cohen, and I. N. Berlin, pp. 378–382. New York: Basic Books.

Douvan, E., and Adelson, G. (1966). *The Adolescent Experience.* New York: Wiley.

Dreikurs, R. (1992). *The Challenge of Parenthood.* New York and revised edition. New York: Plume.

Ekstein, R. (1969a). The child, the teacher and learning. In *From Learning for Love to Love of Learning: Essays on Psychoanalysis and Education,* ed. R. Ekstein and R. L. Motto, pp. 65–78. New York: Brunner/Mazel.

_____ (1969b). The learning process: from learning for love to love of learning. In *From Learning for Love to Love of Learning: Essays on Psychoanalysis and Education,* ed. R. Ekstein and R. L. Motto, pp. 95–106. New York: Brunner/Mazel.

Ekstein, R., and Motto, R. L. (1969). *From Learning for Love to Love of Learning: Essays on Psychoanalysis and Education.* New York: Brunner/Mazel.

Elkind, D. (1984). *The Hurried Child.* New York: Knopf.

_____ (1988). *Miseducation: Preschoolers at Risk.* New York: Knopf.

Elson, M. (1984). Parenthood and the transformation of narcissism. In *Parenthood: A Psychodynamic Perspective,* ed. R. Cohen, B. J. Cohler, and S. H. Weisman, pp. 297–314. New York: Guilford.

_____ (1986). *Self Psychology in Clinical Social Work.* New York: W. W. Norton.

Erikson, E. H. (1950). *Childhood and Society.* New York: W. W. Norton.

_____ (1956). Problems of ego identity. *Journal of the American Psychoanalytic Association:* 4:56–121.

_____ (1959). *Identity and the Life Cycle.* New York: International Universities Press.

Fraiberg, S. (1959). *The Magic Years.* New York: Charles Scribner & Sons.

_____ (1977). *Every Child's Birthright: In Defense of Mothering.* New York: Basic Books.

Freud, A. (1958). Adolescence. In *Psychoanalytic Study of the Child* 13:255–278. New York: International Universities Press.

Garber, B. (1984). Parenting responses in divorce and bereavement of a spouse. In *Parenthood: A Psychodynamic Perspective,* ed. R. Cohen, B. J. Cohler, and S. H. Weisman, pp. 183–203. New York: Guilford.

Gardner, R. A. (1979). Guidance for separated and divorced parents. In *Helping Parents Help Their Children,* ed. L. E. Arnold, pp. 279–291. New York: Brunner/Mazel.

Garmezy, N. (1986). Developmental aspects of children's responses to the stress of separation and loss. In *Depression in Young People,* ed. M. Rutter, C. E. Izard, and P. B. Read, pp. 297–323. New York: Guilford.

Gilligan, C. (1979). Women's place in man's life cycle. *Harvard Educational Review* 49:431–446.

Ginott, H. (1956). *Between Parent and Child.* New York: Avon Books.

Goldstein, J., Freud, A., and Solnit, A. J. (1973). *Beyond the Best Interests of the Child.* New York: Free Press.

Gonzalez-Ramos, G., and Goldstein, E. G. (1989). Child maltreatment: an overview. In *Clinical Social Work with Maltreated Children and Their Families: An Introduction to Practice,* ed. S. M. Ehrenkranz, E. G. Goldstein, L. Goodman, and J. Seinfeld, pp. 3–20. New York: New York University Press.

Hagestad, C. O. (1981). Problems and promises in the social psychology of intergenerational relations. In *Stability and Change in the Family,* ed. R. Fogel et al., pp. 11–46. New York: Academic Press.

Hamburg, B. (1974). Early adolescence: a specific and special stage of the life cycle. In *Coping and Adaptation,* ed. G. Coelho, D. Hamburg, and J. Adams, pp. 101–124. New York: Basic Books.

Harrington, M. (1992). *Women Lawyers: Rewriting the Rules.* New York: Knopf.

Holzman, P. (1980). Discussion—vulnerable youth: hope, despair and renewal. *Adolescent Psychiatry* 8:309–314.

Ianni, F. A. J. (1989). *The Search for Structure: A Report on American Youth Today.* New York: Free Press.

Kagan, J. A. (1971). A conception of early adolescence. *Daedulus* (fall):997–1012.

Kaplan, L. (1984). *Adolescence: The Farewell to Childhood.* New York: Simon & Schuster.

Kessler, J. (1966). *Psychopathology of Childhood.* Englewood Cliffs, NJ: Prentice-Hall.

Kleiman, G. W., and Rosenfeld, A. (1980). *Responsible Parenthood: The Child's Psyche through the Six-Year Pregnancy.* New York: Holt, Rinehart & Winston.

Kohut, H. (1971). *The Analysis of the Self.* New York: International Universities Press.

_____ (1972). Thoughts on narcissism and narcissistic rage. In *Psychoanalytic Study of the Child* 27:360–399. New Haven, CT: Yale University Press.

_____ (1977). *The Restoration of the Self.* New York: International Universities Press.

_____ (1978). *The Search for the Self: Selected Writings of Heinz Kohut, 1950–1978.* New York: International Universities Press.

_____ (1984). *How Does Analysis Cure?* ed. A. Goldberg and P. Stepansky. Chicago: University of Chicago Press.

Laufer, M. (1966). Object loss and mourning during adolescence. In *Psychoanalytic Study of the Child* 2:269–293. New York: International Universities Press.

_____ (1968). The body image, the function of masturbation and adolescence: problems of ownership of the body. In *Psychoanalytic Study of the Child* 28:114–137. New York: International Universities Press.

Lein, L. (1984). Parents at home and on the job. In *Parenthood: A Psychodynamic Perspective,* ed. R. Cohen, B. J. Cohler, and S. H. Weisman, pp. 50–63. New York: Guilford.

Lerner, B. (1982). American education: how are we doing? *Public Interest* 69:59–82.

Lustman, S. (1970). Cultural deprivation: a clinical dimension of education. In *The Psychoanalytic Study of the Child* 25:483–502. New York: International Universities Press.

Mishne, J. (1979). Parental abandonment: a unique form of loss and narcissistic injury. *Clinical Social Work Journal* 7(1):15–33.

_____ (1983). *Clinical Work with Children.* New York: Free Press.

_____ (1986). *Clinical Work with Adolescents.* New York: Free Press.

_____ (1987/1988). *The concept of parental force: academic underachievement.* Unpublished research project for The Spencer Foundation.

_____ (1989). Individual treatment. In *Clinical Social Work with Maltreated Children and Their Families: An Introduction to Practice,* ed. S. M. Ehrenkranz, E. G. Goldstein, L. Goodman, and J. Seinfeld, pp. 38–61. New York: New York University Press.

_____ (1992). The grieving child: manifest and hidden losses in childhood and adolescence. *Child and Adolescent Social Work Journal* 9(6):471–490.

_____ (1993). Primary nocturnal enuresis: a psychodynamic clinical perspective. *Child and Adolescent Social Work Journal* 10(6): 469–495.

Muslin, H. (1984). On the resistance to parenthood: considerations on the self of the father. In *Parenthood: A Psychodynamic Perspective,* ed. R. S. Cohen, B. J. Cohler, and S. H. Weisman, pp. 315–325. New York: Guilford.

Neugarten, B. L. (1979). The middle generation. In *Aging Parents,* ed. P. Ragan, pp. 258–266. Los Angeles: University of Southern California Press.

Noble, B. P. (1993). Interpreting the Family Leave Act. *The New York Times,* August 1, 1993.

Offer, D. (1967). Normal adolescents: interview strategy and selected results. *Archives of General Psychiatry* 17:285–290.

_____ (1984a). Foreword. In *Parenthood: A Psychodynamic Perspective,* ed. R. S. Cohen, B. J. Cohler, and S. H. Weisman, pp. xiii–xvi. New York: Guilford.

_____ (1984b). Culture, values and normalization. In *Normality and the Life Cycle: A Critical Integration,* ed. D. Offer and M. Sabshin, pp. 364–392. New York: Basic Books.

Offer, D., and Sabshin, M. (1963). The psychiatrist and the normal adolescent. *Archives of General Psychiatry* 9:427–432.

Offer, D., Sabshin, M., and Marcus, D. (1965). Clinical evolution of normal adolescents. *American Journal of Psychiatry* 121:864–872.

Oldham, D. (1978). Adolescent turmoil: a myth revisited. In *Adolescent Psychiatry, vol. 6: Developmental and Clinical Studies,* ed. S. Feinstein and P. Giovacchini, pp. 267–279. Chicago: University of Chicago Press.

Paul, N. L. (1970). Parental empathy. In *Parenthood: Its Psychology and Psychopathology,* ed. E. J. Anthony and T. Benedek, pp. 337–352. Boston: Little, Brown & Co.

Rangell, L. (1990). Seventeen: the approach to the portal of adult life. In *New Dimensions in Adult Development,* ed. R. A. Nemiroff and C. A. Colarusso, pp. 3–25. New York: Basic Books.

Richardson, S. T. (1969). The school's role in discipline. In *From Learning for Love to Love of Learning: Essays on Psychoanalysis and Education,* pp. 147–151. New York: Brunner/Mazel.

Ross, J. M. (1984). Fathers in development: an overview of recent contributions. In *Parenthood: A Psychodynamic Perspective,* ed. R. S. Cohen, B. J. Cohler, and S. H. Weisman, pp. 373–390. New York: Guilford.

Russo, N. (1979). Overview: sex roles, fertility and the motherhood mandate. *Psychology of Women Quarterly* 41:7–15.

Rutter, M. (1971). Parent–child separation: psychological effects on children. *Journal of Child Psychiatry and Psychology* 12:233–260.

Rutter, M., Graham, P., Chadwick, O., and Yule, W. (1976). Adolescent turmoil: Fact or fiction? *Journal of Child Psychology and Psychiatry and Allied Disciplines* 17:35–56.

Sarnoff, C. (1976). *Latency.* New York: Jason Aronson.

Spitz, R. (1957). *No and Yes.* New York: International Universities Press.

Stern, D. (1985). *The Interpersonal World of the Infant: A View from Psychoanalysis and Developmental Psychology.* New York: Basic Books.

Taffel, R. (1991). *Parenting by Heart: A William Patrick Book.* New York: Addison-Wesley.

Townsend-Butterworth, D. (1988). Readiness for early childhood schooling. In *Handbook of Clinical Assessment of Children and Adolescents, vol. 1,* ed. C. J. Kestenbaum and D. T. Williams, pp. 315–333. New York: New York University Press.

Wallerstein, J. S., and Kelly, J. B. (1980). *Surviving the Breakup: How Children and Parents Cope with Divorce.* New York: Basic Books.

Weisberger, E. (1987). *When Your Child Needs You.* Bethesda, MD: Adler & Adler.

White, B. L. (1979/1984). *The First Three Years of Life.* (First and later editions). Englewood Cliffs, NJ: Prentice-Hall.

Winn, M. (1985). *The Plug-in Drug.* New York: Viking.

Winnicott, D. W. (1958). The capacity to be alone. In *The Maturational Processes and the Facilitating Environment,* ed. J. Sutherland, pp. 29–36. London: Hogarth Press/International Psychoanalytic Library.

Index

Marcus, D., 87
Mealtime
  discipline and, 22–23
  nursery school, 34
Middle school, 65–83
  family life, 74–83
  normal development in,
    65–69
  parent role, 69–74
Mishne, J., 14, 70, 71, 85, 101,
    105, 175, 209
Motter, R. L., xv
Muslin, H., 217

Neugarten, B. L., 109
Noble, B. P., 144
Nursery school, 33–45
  four-year-olds, 38–39
  parent-child-school fit,
    43–45
  parenting patterns, 39–42
  three-year-olds, 33–38

Offer, D., 74, 87, 93, 163, 164,
    211
Oldham, D., 87

Parent-child relationship. *See
    also* Family life
  college, 109–111
  developmental factors and,
    xvii–xviii, xx
  divorce and, 171–176
  elementary school, 50–54
  high school, 90–94
  homework, 125–141
  middle school, 69–74
  nursery school, 36, 39–42

  perspectives on, 211–217
Parent-guidance approach,
    overview of, xviii–xx
Parenting problems, 187–209
  anxiety, 200–209
  child abuse and neglect,
    195–200
  overview of, 187–190
  spoiled child, 190–195
Parents
  discipline and, 19–29
  inhibitions on, xviii
  pressures on, xvi–xvii
  role of, xv–xvi
  school adjustment,
    preparation for, 11–17
  teachers and, 8–9
Paul, N. L., 216
Peer relationships
  adolescence, 88
  college, 106–107, 116–117
  elementary school, 47–48
  middle school, 66–67
  nursery school, 38–39
Permissiveness
  nursery school, 35
  parenting problems and,
    189–190
Play
  developmental factors and,
    15–16
  elementary school, 50
  nursery school, 36–37
Preschool programs,
    developmental factors and,
    4–5
Puberty, middle school, 65–83
Punishment, discipline and,
    26–27